In God's Presence

By Tara Evans

~Dedication~

I dedicate my first book to all those that pushed me to not give up. To My <u>*Mother*</u>, <u>*daughter*</u>, <u>*brother's*</u>, <u>*sister's*</u> and <u>*friends*</u>. To all my <u>Brother's</u> and <u>Sister's</u> in my church, **<u>New Genesis</u>**.

~Acknowledgements~

Thank you to my entire family, for memories that will last a lifetime.

<u>*Momma, Ruth (Williamson) Evans*</u>, God blessed me with an amazing parent, your love and guidance brought me through my childhood to adulthood and will carry me through my golden years.

<u>*My Daughter, Forrest M. Evans*</u>, I love you! Your birth was the blessing I needed to live. Thank you for always being there for me. Everything you do amazes me, I am so proud of you.

My brother's James, Philip, John, Claude Mark and _Robert_ and _My Sister's Florence, Ramona_ and _Dawn_ thank you all. Within me there is a piece of you all from my smile to my laugh, I see you everyday and I feel you in my heart.

To my Pastor, Eliezer Garcia (my spiritual father) you have been so supportive of me no matter what I try to do. This means the world to me.

To my Pastora, Cindy Garcia (my spiritual mother) thank you so much for guiding me through many issues with no judgment showing me patience, kindness and love. I feel we have a lot in common, just a nod or a smile we seem have our own communication I look up to you. I thank God for you.

Elder Manuel Ortiz, or should I say superman. I don't know how you do it all but I am grateful that you have been so good to allow me to be a part of your family. When I met you, I knew there was something about you that was different and real, no faking. I knew what I saw in you, I wanted (spiritually). You took me under your wing as a little sister and helped me to find who I was seeking. Thank you!

Elder Jennifer Ortiz, I have learned so much from you. Thank you for being the model in which I should walk as a Christian woman.

Elder Carmen Nieves, your love and kind words have got me through so many times when I was ready to give up. Thank you my sister.

To my brother's in the congregation, thank you for looking after me and protecting me as big brother's do, being concerned of my well being and caring about me. This means a lot.

To my sister's in the congregation, thank you for becoming my best friends, always willing to take time out of your busy schedules to be there for me. You all make it so easy to come to you with issues that are sad and joyful. I pray I can be the friend that you all are to me.

<u>*To My dear friend Daphne Wilson-Brown,*</u> the first day we met I knew you were going to be someone special in my life. Thank you for always protecting me like a big sister, always telling me what I needed to hear and not what I wanted to hear. Being truthful and honest at all times. You're the best! Love you.

<u>*To my Boo Boo#2 – Carmen Figueroa,*</u> You're like my second daughter. Just as my Boo Boo#1 I love you with all my heart. You are an amazingly intelligent young lady and I am proud of you.

All the love I have received from you all would take many lifetimes to return. THANK YOU!

~Black & White~

I made the cover of this book and the book in general very plain, white paper black lettering. The reason why I wanted to do this is because when I was a child, we had a grocery store my mom shopped at. In this grocery store I remember there was one whole aisle that was all white and black. Boxed, packaged, and canned food but they all had white labels with black letters. So if you wanted a can of carrots, the food was packaged in a can with a white label and black lettering. Nothing fancy, it's funny because I used to always think to myself "I don't want those carrots. I want the carrots with the pretty picture on the can." Or, "I don't want those corn flakes, there is no picture on the box and no toy inside. How would I get my morning entertainment?" The more I thought about it, as I was thinking of a cover for this book and just the way I wanted the book to be put together. I thought about those carrots and cereal realizing that the outside might be plain but the nutrition was the same on the inside, the carrots are still orange and the corn flakes are still flakes.

I'm kind of looking at it like this, the information on the inside is the same. In the sense that it's the same good information, I'm putting my heart my soul in it and whether I make this big deal of how the book looks or whether I develop the book and market it with just white and black the information is the same.

Some people that go to God I should say, on a personal note I have gone to God and wanted all this fanfare. We go to the churches that are oh so, you know they're new with the nice pews and sanctuaries. The musicians, guitar, drum and piano player's pews stocked with bibles, songbooks and it's just so fancy and impressive.

But then, you have the churches that have almost nothing, they might be a storefront, have a few seats here and there, and all the chairs are different. Maybe they have a couple bibles there to share or you might have a few songbooks scattered with the cover ripped off or whatever the case may be. But when it comes down to it the information is the same, God is the same, the message is the same. So regardless of whether it's all nice and pretty or just plain the way you're going to feel once you leave is the same. You should still receive the same up beat feeling because you're there to hear the word of God.

~Introduction~

Writing this book had its up's and down's. I kind of look at it like, when I was a child. I remember every time I had an orange I would ask my mother to "start it" as I would say. What I meant was to have my mother take the first piece of peel off of the orange. This was so I would be able to continue peeling it on my own until it was done.

I feel God was doing this for me all through this book. I would say Jehovah would you please "start it" and God would give me an amazing idea. God would tell me to run with it or should I say "peel it" until it was done. These words are my words however, seasoned with the love, wisdom and understanding that can only come from God.

I went from thinking I could stand on my own understanding, which does not work. No matter how strong you think you are, God is stronger. No matter how smart or how much wisdom you think you have, God has more. So, doesn't it make sense to do God's will and rely on Him? It seems as if it would make sense, a no brainer! Then why did it take me so long to come to God?

It took me to lose what was the most important to me, finally every possible ounce of it. Myself worth! I am led to remember a conversation I had between myself and a friend. She had this tube of lip gloss and to the eye, all in it seemed gone. My friend would not let this lip gloss go. She would swish that applicator around the container and dab a little lip gloss in that tube on her lips at least twenty times before she made one full application of gloss on her lips. I would laugh at her and say "It's ok, you can throw it away." she would then reply with "No, I paid to much for this and I won't give it up until the last drop is gone." My friend was so funny. (who knew that years later I would gain a lesson from her humor).

I saw myself kind of like that tube of lip gloss, I felt there was no longer anything inside me. I was ready to just throw it away or give up. God saw the little that was still there. God saw I wasn't empty and something good was still in me. I couldn't see hope inside myself It was a blessing to me that God could. Difference is God can replenish and make new.

When I was ready to give up and settle for the life I was living and all the pain I was going through. But God said no! I have more for you, no more tears, no more judgment, no more depression and no more pain. God told me I was worth more than I saw myself to be. God had bought me through His son Jesus Christ (1Corinthians 6:20) and He lifted me up from the ashes to beauty.

The more I think of it, the more I realized, along my journey God has tried on many occasions to turn me around. I chose to ignore God, accepting the blessing when they came but doing nothing more to please God and show Him that I was grateful.

Table of Contents:

Dedication	1
Acknowledgements	1-4
Black & White	5-7
Introduction	8-11

THE BEGINNING

1. <u>17 – Moving away from home</u>

- Ok, where do I start?   18-30
- Becoming Tara   31-33

2. *One night stands vs. long-term no where vs. boyfriends/relationships*

- Relationships   34–40
- Circle Time   41–44
- Fornication/Sexually Immoral   45-53
- Another Piece of the Puzzle   54-54
- Draw a line   55–57

THE EXTREME TRUTH

3. *Psych ward*

- Past view on men   59–60
- Show and Share (explicit)   60–63
- Animal   64–66
- Better   67–70
- My Testimony   71–94
- Presentation   95–98

4. *Stumble*

- Hot Mess   99-104
- Mr. Right   105–112
- My Condition   113–117

- Side Chick — 118-122

THE GLORY OF GOD REVEALED!

5. *God*

- Depression — 124-127
- Packages — 128-133
- Amusement Park — 134-138

6. *What I learned*

- Afro — 139-140
- Back in the Day — 141-144
- Giving It Away — 145-150

- Red Rover, Red Rover   151-153
- Wow! Pow! Slap!   154-160
- Dark to Light   161-162

In Conclusion   163-165

Scriptures used   167-169

Bible used- English Standard Version (ESV)   170-170

THE BEGINNING

1. Moving away from home 17

~Ok, where do I start? ~

Let me start from somewhere close to the beginning. I had a good childhood, I remember as far back as early grade school. Family, friends, school, summer and Christmas vacations. I just remember a different time like a painting, everything seemingly perfect. Children playing outside, in the summer hop scotch. There was always at least a half dozen little girls and sometimes boys enjoying in the fun. We would all play red light green light, about fifteen to twenty of us stopping and going, freezing in sometimes the funniest poses. Sledding in the winter, again dozens of us on the hill, waiting for our turn to slide down wind whipping in our faces hearts racing faces frozen by time we got to the bottom. Making snowmen and the occasional snow women, going to each other's apartments to get a carrot for the nose, hats, scarf's, and something for the eyes.

Oh the times we had, no Facebook, tweeting, sharing, pinning or texting to get in the way of good ole interaction between people. I even had a best friend, my doll Pat. She meant the world to me, I would tell her everything. How I felt, my inner most secrets. Don't get me wrong, I had schoolmates and friends I played outside with but Pat was my most cherished friend.

Pat was African American, mocha brown colored the facial features were not African American they were Caucasian. Back in the 70's dolls of color only had color to show the race not the facial feature like the dolls of today. Pat had a soft body but her arms, legs and head were plastic. She also had hair, not just painted on. Last but not least Pat had eyes that closed when she laid down and opened when sitting up. I love and miss Pat.

Times have truly changed! Don't get me wrong life wasn't perfect but it was good. I lived with my mother and siblings, I am the last child of ten children. However, at this time only eight of us lived with my Mom. I love my mother with all of my heart, she has taught me so much in life.

My Mom is the essence of stability and responsibility. A woman that loves all her children unconditionally. My mother is not a woman who is going to give me random kisses and hugs as a form of love. Her love was shown more in the way she took care of me. Her love came in her sacrifice, her willingness to do with out for herself, even her basic needs.

I remember when I was seventeen. Not long after I started working in the bakery shop at the mall. Unfortunately, I had gained a bit of weight. The button on my favorite blue jean, a lined, slightly flared at the bottom skirt had popped off. Instead of giving up and admitting that the skirt was just too tight in the mid-section. I figured that maybe if I'd use a safety pin, "I thought a safety pin, yeah, that should do the trick". Denying to myself the weight I had gained, I went downstairs to get a safety pin from my mom. I knew Mama had one. My mother use to wear them on the scoop neck collars of her nightdress. It was unusual this morning that she didn't have one pinned to her nightdress. Mama told me to go upstairs to her bedroom, in the short dresser she said in the very middle drawer there would be a box of safety pins.

My mother's dresser had nine small dresser drawers lined up in three's, across and down. I, being the half-listening teenager that I was, I went in the middle drawer on the right hand side of the dresser, not in the very middle as I was told. I reached into the right hand middle dresser drawer and pulled out what I thought was a white piece of material. I wondered, "Why would she have this in her dresser drawer?" Until I looked closer.

I was holding in my hand not just material

but my mother's underwear. It was the most pitiful thing I had ever seen. As I unfolded them, I noticed that her underwear didn't have elastic on the waist, or around the legs. They were worn to the point where holes were all over. Some of the holes were so big you couldn't tell the difference between the holes and the openings for the legs. All of her underwear were like this. As I looked at my mother's underwear, tears swelled in my eyes. All I could think of was how selfish I had been how I had only thought of myself all the time. None of my underwear looked like that; as matter of fact, I never had anything worn as badly as that underwear. My mother had made sure we had everything we needed and most of what we really wanted. I realized at that moment how wonderful a mother I have and how much respect I have for her. I understood my mother without knowing it, my mother had showed me the definition of what the word "mother" really means.

My mom was not a frivolous woman. Every

penny went to us kids; she did not spend unnecessarily on herself, let alone on anyone that was not one of us kids. We had more than enough. My mother didn't just give us the necessities; she gave us a lot of the things we wanted as well. As a mother myself I can't imagine how she did it. She would make sure we had two or three full outfits for Easter.

Christmas was multiplied by so much; I remember one Christmas that sticks out in my mind. In the apartment that we lived in my bedroom was down the hall in the back. Christmas morning, I would wake up and sneak down the hall and come around the corner to the living room. There was this one Christmas specifically. I remember the tree, the light of the moon was coming through the curtain and it hit the tinsel on the tree just right. There was a snow type effect on the tree like when the light of the moon hits the snow it looks kind of bluish, that's how the tree looked. The presents seemed to flow from the tree in the corner to the middle of the room. Now understand, my mother had several children and even at that time, several of us lived in the house. And yet, she managed to get multiple gifts for each of us. It was just amazing, my mother showed her love in different ways.

She baked and cooked all by scratch. She showed her love in the way she fed us, the way she clothed us, the way she sacrificed for us. She did her best so we didn't want for anything, that is how my mother showed her love. My mother sacrificed for us, I believe to the point of her own happiness. Giving up the possibility of someone in her life to live her golden years with, someone to cherish her as she deserves. My mother took her responsibility of being a parent extremely serious and I am grateful for that. God gave me the most amazing mother.

There was always something going on in my house, music, conversations, teasing and of course a lot of love. My father was not in the household. My mother and father weren't married. I saw my father once in a while growing up and less and less as the years went on. You know how some women say, "I am my children's mother and father". I never saw my mother as a father to me. However, I saw her, as I said before an amazing mother. It wasn't her job to be my father that job belonged to my father and he didn't do it. Do I hold a grudge? At times, however, I love my father just the same because that's who he is to me. I think of why a call my father "pop", it's because it's what I can handle calling my father. I can't call him dad, father or daddy because all those words to me imply that he was an active participate in my life in my upbringing. That he did something that had in someway made impression on my life that was positive. Basically those titles, in my opinion belong to a man that raised his children. My Father was not there for me and as an adult this effects me greatly. Out of the three children he has, I am the one he shows the least care for.

I guess I was a lot angrier with him than I thought. I stated I didn't really have a grudge. I don't really have a grudge (sometimes). I have packed down in my soul, anger for this man that is my biological father. I didn't realize how much he really affected my life as an adult. I do however love him, and I have come to realize that no matter how I felt or feel. I must obey what God's word is on the issue of father's.

<u>In Deuteronomy 5:16 states, Honor your father and your mother, as the LORD your God commanded you, that your days may be long, and that it may go well with you in the land that the LORD your God is giving you.</u>

We moved from the only home I knew just as I started Jr. high school. I am dating myself, we called it Jr. high now it's middle school. That time in my life was good as well. I remember going to my cousin's house to play double-dutch and even then dozens of us were outside playing. That was also the time when break dancing was popular. Watching kids battle each other on a piece of card board. There was always kids that blew your mind with what they could do. Looking back, it was like a sport all of it's own. The long and short of it was, I was happy or at least what I thought happiness was to be. No real care in the world.

Next, high school. A time in my life where things started to change, but for the good. A time to grow and learn about life, not just school. A time for more than reading, writing and arithmetic, now the bird's and the bee's were a more prevalent aspect in my life. "He's so cute", was really the only qualification needed, when I was in high school. Oh, I forgot one other qualification, did I 'like him' or 'like him, like him?' The second 'like' was the deal maker. In high school, there were about six or seven girls pregnant and not married. Maybe half had guys that were going to stay and take responsibility, these guys were always with their girls and did all they could for them, well as much as I could see. But what about the others?

Going through that whole experience alone,

that's rough. I did it alone and it was no picnic (I had my daughter at the age of twenty-two). Granted, yes I had my sister and a friend there but that is not the same as the father of the child you are carrying being there for you.

Graduation day, this is the day I believed my life would change. No longer a child but an adult, able to make my own choices. Without my mother's consent, I now am a woman! Well, as long as I am not under mommies' roof. Other than that, I am now a full grown woman!! So I thought. I decided after graduation it was time to spread my wings and go live with my sister (same state different city). My sister, only nine years older but, wow so cosmopolitan. She knew everything! Living and doing as she pleased, seemed great. Now that's how a woman lives and now I was a woman. This is my new life; no more being told what to do. No more rules, life was going to be a party.... No, reality set in soon after I got there. Rules are in every house and my sister didn't drag her feet on telling me what those rules were. It only took a couple of weeks for me to find a job and fulfill the obligations in my sister's household. I really liked living with my sister. She just seemed so together, I felt there were so many things I could learn from her. Just as I did when we were kids. I had a strong bond with my sister from childhood.

I lived with my sister for less than a month, when my life completely changed. I was raped and I was still a virgin. My identity changed, my sense of security changed. How I would see myself, how I would love myself and how I would treat myself. How I would allow men to see me and treat me. Why? Because this is the changing point in my life when I lost myself worth. When all the things I dreamed of growing up were now shattered.

My sister had a "friend", that is what you call a man who you are having a casual sexual thing with. We as women confuse ourselves to believe there is a real relationship. When it ends we can't understand, why. Now, why can't we understand why? We make no commitment with this man, no real foundation in the somewhat called "relationship". However, we still are confused at times and can't understand what happened. I didn't tell her about this until years later, I was afraid she would be mad at me. Most of all I was afraid of losing her love. I am so sorry, I should have known better, please forgive me.

~Becoming Tara~

I remember before I was raped and I hate to say that phase "before I was raped". I remember when I came into my own identity I felt I was pretty, I liked myself and respected myself. I remember having a friend that wanted me to kind of messed around with a friend that she had messed around with. I don't know if she felt so guilty, dirty or whatever for doing what she did, that she wanted me to do it as well. Who knows, we were only twelve... I remember being very strong in saying no and not being pressured into it.

I also remember the same friend had another friend. We were all sitting in the bathroom at a local mall and they pulled out a cigarette. Now this dates me because you can't smoke a cigarette in the bathroom or any public place now. But then you could, or should I say it wasn't as hard to be sneaky about it. Again, we were in the bathroom and they pulled out a cigarette, passing it back and forth the girl handed it to me. I made very clear to her "No!" I remember her telling me while they were smoking if I wanted to be a part of the group I would have to smoke too. I let her know that I didn't need to be a part of a group that's trying to decide what I was going or not going to do. I was very strong in knowing what I wanted.

Another time I went on a bike ride with a guy. He was such a nice guy I liked him he was very sweet but, I didn't want to do what he wanted to do. He was upset and called me a baby and a lot of other not so nice names. I still felt secure with myself to know that he's a nice guy but he's not the guy I want to give any of that to, he wasn't that special to me and I wanted to save that for the one I love.

You see I had a romantic notion of what love was and I wanted to wait. There were other incidences because of course as I grew up, I interacted with boys and I knew they wanted to be with me or touch me or whatever. I just remember telling at least half a dozen of them specifically that I was strong in my convictions. That's what I remember, that I was okay with myself I felt good about me. I wasn't afraid to tell someone how I felt and I held my head up high, taking in all the criticism. I wanted certain things for myself and I was okay with saying that.

I think what makes me angry is that prior to being raped. I told boys "No!", I said no to them. I told them I wanted to wait until I was in love. But the man that raped me just took it from me. Sometimes I heavily regret saying no, because at least my first time would have been with someone I liked. Instead of someone I feared for many years.

2. One night stands vs. long-term no where vs. boyfriends/relationships

~Relationships~

On Facebook, I saw a post from one of my friends and it stated something on the lines of this:

~Your kids shouldn't meet every man you date & neither should your vagina~

I thought for a moment, then all I could do was laugh at this post. I could see the point that was trying to be made but I felt more should be said. I agreed for some not for all.

Let me explain how my old way of thinking agreed. Meaning, you don't need to have every guy you have a date with be introduced to your children. Why? Because they aren't all men you want to have a relationship with. However, my new way of thinking (putting God first). God's will and teachings tell me if he is not marriage material and you know that up front, then why are you dating him in the first place?

A funny comment on Facebook turned into a thought provoking question for me to really examine. Now, as for the second part regarding vagina's, that shouldn't be an issue if you are not married. Meaning, no date should meet your vagina because that special part of a relationship that is saved for your husband.

1Corinthians 6:18-20 18-Flee from sexual immorality. Every other sin a person commits is outside the body, but the sexually immoral person sins against his own body. 19-Or do you not know that your body is a temple of the Holy Spirit within you, whom you have from God? You are not your own, 20-for you were bought with a price. So glorify God in your body.

When I read this scripture I notice it doesn't make this point for just women. Gentlemen, you are just as responsible to refrain as women. If you know things are going too far and this is going to make you have negative thoughts regarding someone that you may like, take the lead and say "Maybe it's best we wait and get to know each other better." Instead of giving into something that will bring unpleasant consequences.

Just because men don't seem to be accountable in the world regarding sex, to God they are. This should make you think about trying to be with every Mary Jane and Sue, Tom, Dick and Harry or "Sowing your wild oats" (as the sayings go). The world encourages the boys to be with as many girls as possible, to be seen as the man, the stud. The thought is to put on a condom and all is fine. The world does not tell their girls this. Have as many men as you can before you choose that one man and be stuck with the same ole stuff everyday. NO! The world doesn't say this, there is one standard for men and one for women. God However, says both are responsible to "Honor God with your body_" (1 Corinthians 6:20)_. That's truly refreshing.

Then I thought to myself: Why is it that some women pick up with just any man and make them a part of their lives? I ask myself "Why don't we all look for a man that will treat us like a queen?" The question in my head is, "Why??" I have come to a conclusion that we as women (some not all) can't recognize when a man is treating us good or bad. Again, why? Because how can we, when we were never treated like a princess. If your father never treated you as a princess and showed you (by his treatment to your mother) how a queen should be treated, then I ask how would a good portion of us know? I sure didn't.

The belief is, he'll come around and be the man/husband I know he can be. But, does he know what kind of man he can be? Is the same issue for women as for men? The lack of being shown or lack of guidance. And then I think, is that really for you or for him to recognize and apply? I scratch my head at this and mainly because I did it for years. Thinking a man would change just because I loved him, and for no other reason.

However, when you show a man love that is God's love, a love that is above all; then there is a chance he could change based on you being the Christian he see's. The way you treat him, recognizing he is the head of the household. Showing him respect and submitting to his decisions.

Ephesians 5:22-33 tells us this:

22-Wives, submit to your own husbands, as to the Lord. 23-For the husband is the head of the wife even as Christ is the head of the church, his body, and is himself its Savior. 24-Now as the church submits to Christ, so also wives should submit in everything to their husbands. 25-

Husbands, love your wives, as Christ loved the church and gave himself up for her, 26-that he might sanctify her, having cleansed her by the washing of water with the word, 27-so that he might present the church to himself in splendor, without spot or wrinkle or any such thing, that she might be holy and without blemish. 28-In the same way husbands should love their wives as their own bodies. He who loves his wife loves himself. 29-For no one ever hated his own flesh, but nourishes and cherishes it, just as Christ does the church, 30-because we are members of his body. 31- "Therefore a man shall leave his father and mother and hold fast to his wife, and the two shall become one flesh." 32- This mystery is profound, and I am saying that it refers to Christ and the church. 33-However, let each one of you love his wife as himself, and let the wife see that she respects her husband

However, every man/husband won't change based on this. As a Christian, your first thought should be to marry a Christian. But, if you are married prior to being a Christian 1 Corinthians states.

1Corinthians 7:13-14 13-If any woman has a husband who is an unbeliever, and he consents to live with her, she should not divorce him. 14- For the unbelieving husband is made holy because of his wife, and unbelieving wife is made holy because of her husband. Otherwise your children would be unclean, but as it is, they are holy.

~Circle Time~

One of the earliest memories I have, speaking of marriage was way back in grade school. I remember that event this way. My most favorite teacher in the world, rounded us up for circle time. We all moved our chairs in a circle, then the teacher asked this question of us. "What do you want to be when you grow up?" Wow! Yes!! Just the question I have been wanting to hear! My mouth started to salivate, you know when you're so excited to share your mouth salivates right at the corners. I knew what I was going to say. As matter of fact, me and a friend in class was just talking about this the day before.

Now the world will know what my hopes and dreams will be. What I will accomplish in my life, the big woman I will become. What I, Tara R. Evans will be when I grow up. My mind kind of drifting off, I could see myself in my wonder woman underroos with my hands on my hips, looking up to the sky, Trumpets sounding like in the movies. Also a slight breeze blowing my hair and cape, you can't forget that it really makes the whole vision.

Ok, now we are starting up. Round the circle we go! I heard answers like doctors, lawyers, nurses, business owners, and judges just to name a few. The teacher said "Wonderful", as she clapped her hands together. Another "Just wonderful", she always encouraged the class. This is what made me like her so much. Then it came to be my turn, "Tara what would you like to be when you grow up?" I took a deep breath, because this was important stuff. Exhaled and stated "A ballet dancer", I stole my friends thunder by adding her into mine. She did not seem to mind, but all in all I should have allowed her to have her own moment.

Now the last girls turn, I don't remember her name but I do remember her. She was a soft spoken girl; I remember she always had a smile on her face even when she was sad. The same question was asked of her as the rest of us. Her answer however was so different, an answer I would never have thought of. She stated to the teacher when she grew up she wanted to become a wife and a mother. "WHAT!!!! This is an outrage!" I thought to myself but I know my facial expression showed what I was thinking. I blurted out, "That's not the right answer, that's not what was asked!" My teacher nicely explained to me that was what she wanted and there was nothing wrong with her answer. Hmm, I wasn't buying it. I remember being angry for days about this.

At home I told my sister but, she agreed with the teacher and the girl. I didn't get it. Why couldn't I wrap my head around this? Because up till that point in my life, I thought everyone got married and had children. Almost like, you really did not have a choice. But at some point it just happened. I had grown up on fairy tale's all my life. Well, up to that time in my life and I truly believed that it would just be. I did not need to do anything for it or even want it. Marriage and children would just happen on it's own.

So I expressed this savvy bit of information to my sister because I didn't think she knew. With confidence in my voice and boldness in my heart I told her about what I knew. My sister smiled at me, as only she could and held me, explaining that wasn't the way it was. How when it was my time, I would have choices. Not every person wants marriage and children. So I asked "How would I know?" "Well Tara," she carefully started the conversation, "You will know if he is the person for you because you will love him." Love? Ah another piece of the puzzle, ummmm. Anything more at that time would have been too much for me to handle, you see I was only seven.

~Fornication/Sexually Immoral~

Fornication/Sexually Immoral, now people think that fornication/Sexually Immoral behavior isn't an issue or a negative action, but it is. Fornication/Sexual immorality is a sin. A sin that was going to prevent me from inheriting the kingdom of God.

> *1Corinthians 6:9-10   9-Or do you not know that the unrighteous will not inherit the kingdom of God? Do not be deceived: neither the sexually immoral, nor idolaters, nor adulterers, nor men who practice homosexuality, 10-nor thieves, nor the greedy, nor drunkards, nor revilers, nor swindlers will inherit the kingdom of God.*

So when I speak of turning my life around because, in my past I fornicated/sexually immoral; I would always have someone say to me "You didn't do anything wrong so why are you turning your life around?" Or "I don't understand you're just having sex." A friend of mine told me once, "You're not dating anyone, you're not in a relationship, you're not married and you're not cheating on anyone. So who are you really hurting? Whose business is it, who you have sex with? No one has the right to know! It's your body it's your right to do with it as you please. Just be careful!" This comment reminds me of something my sister would say, "Tara that's ghetto logic, you're better than that". What she meant was that is your own logic that comes from nowhere, no facts and no research words said in the moment.

This is what the world believes and what I use to believe. The enemy brainwashed me to think I was the owner of me. That I need to go along with the times, as if God had changed and my actions did not matter. My response is, "It's God's business and it is He who has every right to know." (1Corinthians 6:18-20 states)

> *1 Corinthians 6:18-20   18-Flee from sexual immorality. Every other sin a person commits is outside the body, but the sexually immoral person sins against his own body. 19- Or do you not know that your body is a temple of the Holy Spirit within you, whom you have from God? You are not your own, 20-for you were bought with a price. So glorify God in your body*

When I was fornicating, not only did I sin against God, I sinned against myself as well. I never thought it was possible to sin against myself, I was confused about that. But then, I thought of all the pain and stress this behavior has caused me. The mental strain, self loathing, and extreme low self esteem and self worth. When I took the time to think on a reasonable level and not emotional, I could see God was trying to protect me from this pain. If I had only listened, it doesn't matter whether I was just out there giving it away or if I was in a relationship or anything in between. Nowadays, what people call each other in a relationship varies and can get quite colorful in language.

I thought about prostitution and how the world sees prostitution as a bad thing. Well of course, until someone prominent uses the services. It's very simple, one party provides the sexual services were the other party provides the finance. That's the long and short of the definition of prostitution. It hurt me to come to realize that my relationships weren't much different. It was at this time I had to face the facts as hurtful and shameful as it was. Whether I give it away to a boyfriend or one-night stand or who knows who, the sin is still fornication. Which means, I was having intimate sexual intercourse with someone that was not my spouse.

Whatever I wanted to call it, whatever excuse I wanted to make it is still fornication. Which means, I was sinning against the one who loved me the most. I sinned against God! I had to take sides, I needed to make a decision. You can't serve two masters as it says in the bible.

Matthew 6:24 states. 24- "No one can serve two masters, for either he will hate the one and love the other, or he will be devoted to the one and despise the other. You cannot serve God and money.

You can't serve the world and serve Jehovah. It can't happen, so I had to make a decision. Do I want to please Jehovah God or do I want to please the world and the enemy who lies with in it? Which way was I going to go? I had to stop and think, what is the reason why I'm so passionate about this subject? Because it's something that people just don't realize, especially women. And you know we feel it is our business, our body, it's our "what have you" and it's not. If I wanted to serve Jehovah, I wanted to please Jehovah and I want to do His will, I have to keep myself chase. I have to, but the world was telling me that it is my body, it's my business. It's my everything however, the bible says different and I had to think about that. I think about how much happier I am right now yes, lonely at times granted sad because of it. However, all in all I am so much happier than I was running around trying to find a man.

I think what kills me about the whole thing is that women think that, hmmm let me think of how I want to say this. Well, women and men, you have men that will give money so that she "Puts out" and then, you have women that will put out if money is given. This is an acceptable part of a relationship. I don't want that in my relationship. I don't want to feel like I'm putting out for my man to pay the bills. But at times in the past I felt my relationships were just that. To do this and that so he pays the bills and gives me gifts and things like that. So sex becomes a function. I don't want that to be the main aspect, or any aspect of my relationship. It is supposed to be a loving relationship. But if I don't learn God's will, that is the type of relationship I would end up in. God tells me there is more.

My whole mind frame has changed. In the past, I wanted to go out on a date. I wanted to dress up and that was the jest of it. But my mind now, I am thinking to myself "If it's not going to lead to something or the intension isn't going to lead to something positive, something serious. Leading to marriage, then I am not interested in as much as a date. I am just not interested in wasting anyone's time and especially not wasting mine." It's a good feeling. I don't want that superficial type of relationship I've had before.

See, what made me uneasy in my past was the assumption that if you are a decent looking woman, then you need someone to take care of you to maintain. The premise is, you're going to use this man and get whatever there is to get from him. My **pride** is saying, (because the truth is God revealed different) no man in this world have I ever used in this manner and that is one thing I can say I am so proud of. I didn't fall to the point that I felt I needed to use a man, or stayed with a man. Because I was using him to pay my bills. I never did that but I did use men in other ways. Now, I am not going to say that there weren't men that stayed with me to have sex. But, I can assure you I have never stayed with a man and used him for his money. Because there has never been a man, and there will never be a man that I need his money. That I need him to buy me things because I am the type of person that I will get what I need for myself. I have always been that way and presently now and in the future.

I know that if I ask God, He will provide for me. Providing the things I need that are in His will. I know that God will always be with me to provide the tools needed for each task at hand. God gives me the strength, power and the wisdom to be able to take care of it as long as it is within His will. I definitely am not going to ask for something that He does not condone. So there is nothing I need that would require me to subject or degrade myself for anyone to take care of me in that manner. Men, you don't need to be desperate for fear that this woman is so above you or so fantastic that you're going to pay her in a sense to stay with you. Because when it really comes down to it, that's what you are doing if she is not willing to stay on her own. She is probably not the woman for you. If a man is not willing to stay with me because he loves me and truly wants to be with me. Willing to be patient and wait to marry me. If not, then he's not the right man for me.

But all in all if God is not firmly placed in my relationship it's not going to work the way I want it to, it's not going to work in the wholesome loving way that a relationship needs to work. If everyone doesn't know where they belong and everyone isn't participating in their role within that relationship, then there will always be bumps and pitfalls. You will have things happen that are unnecessary because two people are not on the same page. The blessing for me is to be able to recognize when someone is not for me and move on.

~Another piece of the puzzle~

In the back of my mind was always, "Give the man I am with what he wants, so it's not taken from me." A sick sense of security and comfort, at least he will stay for a little while. Because I gave sex to this man I felt I was the one in control. But reality is when I sinned, because fornication is a sin, the one in control is the enemy. The enemy has no boundary's, there are no lines he won't cross he will mislead you at any chance he gets. The enemy doesn't care that he is painfully touching your very soul. The bible tells us this:

> *1Peter 5:8 8-Be sober- minded; be watchful. Your adversary the devil prowls around like a roaring lion, seeking someone to devour.*

~Drawing a line~

From day one, after being sexually violated, I didn't know myself worth and I accepted my treatment from men as they wanted to treat me. Why did I allow this? Because I never drew a line in the sand, so to speak. Yes, a simple line in the sand. In other words, I never put up a limit as to the behavior that I was not willing to accept. Trying to do this on my own never worked. I would stand up for my beliefs. I know now however, I did not know then. But then the enemy would put someone I thought was so much better than the rest in my path. Someone that I thought I wasn't good enough for, there's when the self worth comes into play, and I would give in to this man. I would go back to accepting whatever he was willing to give. Like, showing up when he felt like it day or night. Coming home to him sitting on my couch. Stupid me gave him a key, what did I expect. Eating my food that sometimes was not enough for me and my daughter, let alone him. But he did not seem to care when there was no more, he would just go home. Meaning when the food was gone, the cable turned off, the heat not working or anything else wrong in the apartment, he would abandon me.

As much as I would like to play the victim, the blame lies with me. I allowed this to happen, because I thought very little of myself and I believed he was better than me and I didn't want to lose him. After the short honeymoon period it would turn ugly just like before. A lot of us have gone through this whether we want to admit it or not. For me, admitting this was one of the first steps for me to open my life to God. There was a time I just wanted to be so strong. I never wanted to let anyone see I was weak at times, really at any time. Showing I didn't have it all together in relationships, finances, friendships to mention a few. I had to come to grips that I needed help at this point in my life. We are not perfect by any means. By just merely making that statement before a conversation, doesn't mean we believe ourselves. You know what I mean, when you are in a conversation and one of the ladies say "I know I am not perfect but...", Then she says something that even she found hard to believe. What is good to know is God knows we are not perfect and He is not concerned of that! God passes no judgment. Wow! Isn't that refreshing to know? That was definitely refreshing for me to know. For a long time, I was afraid to go to God. To be in His presences terrified me. Why? Because I wasn't handling my business in the correct way. I knew it and God knew it too. God never gave up on me and He has not given up on you either! God loves us no matter what and who we are. God sees the worthiness in us, the strength, the loving, the caring, the kindness, and the intelligence even when we don't see it.

THE EXTREME TRUTH

3. *Psych ward*
~Past view on men~

My past view of men, I used to think that men were pretty much useless. I thought men had only two purposes in life for women, money and sex. So in my narrow mindedness I felt he needed to "throw down" (perform well sexually) in the bedroom and help me financially. Meaning he gave me money here or there. Because, I knew he was going creep in my bed. So, I felt I was entitled to some help here and again. Other than that, that's all they were worth in the past for me. So why am I so shocked that I was viewed in a negative way? That was a good man in my opinion. At the time I felt a bad one was that man that crept up in my bed, left things (meaning he got me pregnant) and now I would have children by someone that really does not care.

This way of thinking comes from being hurt so many times, being disappointed so many times, but I put myself in that position. Because I didn't ask for anything in the way of a good man or relationship I never got anything. I got exactly what I asked for which was nothing. This is where my self-worth needed to be elevated, this is when I needed to think better about me. To get what I feel I deserve in life. Not just with a man and a relationship, but with my finances, child, home, friendships, coworkers and promotions. Because I didn't ask, I didn't get and that is the bottom line. I see my thinking was wrong. The more I asked for nothing the worse the quality of man came in my life. Finally, the way I saw myself was completely shot. I hated me more than anything in the world!

~~~~~~~

This is how I felt, I wrote this January 2014. I hated myself so much, I viewed myself as a dog.

I titled the hate I had for myself:

~Show and Share~

At this time in my life I should be celebrating my triumphs, successes, loves, job, friends and families. But instead I feel so WORTHLESS. A failure within my family, as a parent, a sister and daughter. Completely worthless as a woman, having and deserving no respect or love.

One night a nightmare overwhelmed my dreams. A man dressing me up to show and share with his friends. ~Walking behind with a leash around my neck "Purr like a cat b****, know your place" ~Don't miss a step or make him look bad. Fine fine clothes, cars and house, because what happens here would never make it a home.

All in the game arrive with there own cats on leashes. Whose b**** is the baddest? A handful for a couple dozen. Night of showing is done now the real nightmare begins. The new dog fight. So many looked, watched and wanted. He invited them back. NOW SHOW WHAT YOU REALLY ARE TO HIM!!!!!!!

Stripped of all but the leash. Tug on the leash. ~Sit here/in and out/up and down! He always starts the nightmare, ~masks, especially on me. I must seem like I am enjoying it. ~Pants down, passing around. One pulls on the leash, "Bounce on that B****!"

Every day conversation fills the air while each takes their turn. "Your b**** is tight, good b****!" No not tight, Swollen! It doesn't hurt anymore. No feelings at all just empty. No body or soul. The first sign of blood there is a sick sense of mercy. By the leash, pulled by the neck. Locked in a room, a bucket and blanket. a dirty rag to wipe between. Until it's time to show and share again.

I woke sobbing, shaking and vomiting in my

thinking I managed to reduce myself to an animal. Less than human. Believing this is who I am, no doubt in my mind this was me. My life to come until I was completely useless to anyone, especially myself.

~Animal~

At one point in my life, I felt as if I wasn't human. Feeling worthless, feeling as I didn't matter. Wasn't concerned about what someone looked like as long as the inside was basically decent. And still I really wasn't asking for much, or receiving much. After the rape I felt as if it didn't matter. Because in my now sick thinking, any man, if he wanted me sexually could overpower me and take what he wanted. So I felt like physically I wasn't protected, however my heart was protected. He couldn't have that and my mind was protected, he couldn't have that. I thought at one point my soul was protected, but I found that wasn't true. The enemy took that, little by little. God gave my soul back to me all at one time and made me completely whole.

I got to a point that I felt like an animal and no longer a human. A slave with no control over myself, my body or my soul. I had to keep something personal, that's the part that was so hard for me to share. That's why my walls emotionally were always up. Until I met a man I thought was so special, different from the rest so I thought. Not sure if it was him or what it was but I let those walls down, it almost cost me my life. Although I wasn't a prostitute I felt like I had the mentality of a prostitute. I gave physically for whatever reason. There was an intense emotional part of me that I never gave that I only wanted to give to someone I knew and loved.

Loving someone was so hard to do because trust is an issue for me. I did not love this man but I did trust him. He was the first person, I should say man (relationship) that I trusted. There may be a handful of people in general, friends and family that I trust. The people I will give my all to, where no walls exist. These are the people that see the whole me, no facade. But then I ask myself, "Why this man?" I didn't love him, he didn't earn my trust I just gave him my trust, but why him? I really don't know. However, I can say the outcome was a blessing. When he disappointed me it caused me to go into an extreme depression and forced me to listen to God. God showed me my worth, no one else could have done that, not even me. I realized that I need God in my life so in that sense I'm very grateful to have met this man that almost caused me to kill myself. You will understand in my testimony.

~Better~

I can't explain how mangled my mind was in the past. So mangled so incredibly mangled, my thoughts were completely unrealistic. Crazy, violent and sexual. These were just horrible horrible thoughts that not only made me depressed but afraid. I can't explain why I was in another church sect for five years and never had a personal intimate relationship with God. I can't explain, that doesn't make sense to me.

Let me explain what I do know about how my mental state was. I see it like being in a bad car accident. Now in this accident, my leg is inter twined with a piece of the car, lodged in well. At that point what do you do? How do you get free? You go to the hospital and the doctor just leaves the piece of car in your leg. The doctor says "You know what, I'm just going to leave that there, you will be ok. Unless, you are willing to lose the leg." So what do you do, just walk around with that piece of car in your leg? I got a strong feeling that's going to be hard to get a pair of panty hose over. I'm just saying. But when I thought about it, that's what I did. I was inter-mangled with my thoughts and my past. With all the things that were going on it was almost like it was wedged in or fused together. The only way to get rid of that, the only way to brake free was to sever some of the things, people and places from my past. To move on to my future, like in the accident example, I'm not going to walk around with a piece of car in my leg just because I am afraid to lose my leg. I don't want to lose my leg no matter what. Even if it makes you better? So I walk around with that piece of car in my leg rather than lose it.

To have a better life without the leg than to stumble and fall with the leg attached to the piece of car.

Mark 9:43-47 states: 43-And if your hand causes you to sin, cut it off. It is better for you to enter life crippled than with two hands to go to hell, to the unquenchable fire. 45-And if your foot causes you to sin, cut it off. It is better for you to enter life lame than with two feet to be thrown into hell. 47-And if your eye causes you to sin, tear it out. It is better for you to enter the kingdom of God with one eye than with two eyes to be thrown into hell

That's how my past was. I was so afraid of losing, not even knowing what I was afraid of losing, but I was afraid just the same. And I held on to all these bad habits, bad feeling and bad thoughts thinking if I let go I would lose my personality. If I severed those parts of me that I have grown accustomed to then who would I be? What was going to happen to me? I was so afraid of getting better I was willing to stay unhealthy so afraid to get healthy, mentally. I was just so use to it and I thought this is just me, who I was and unable to change. Maybe a car accident with a piece of the car attached to my leg is not the best example, but there are people that have issues with their leg or arm some body part that is pretty much poisoning them. And they would rather hold on to that and continue to be poisoned, continue to have that pain than to just sever it move on and live a better, happier, joyful life. And that's what I needed to do with my mental health.

~My Testimony~

I will start off by saying before attending New Genesis, I was very depressed. Depression, coupled with low self esteem, in all honestly – I loathed myself! The inside of me, completely shattered. I spent my adult life being used by men, I must say. I allowed it, if you do not know your worth it's easy for this to happen. When I was of no more use, sexually, I would be crumpled up and thrown away like a piece of folded blank white paper. Time taught me to be cold and hard.

I started to think I should get something out of the relationship I was in at the time, instead of always being the one with a broken heart at the end. But that wasn't me, so I continued to be the one that got hurt the most. I learned how to somewhat protect my self at least with my appearance on the outside, inside I was a hot mess. I also learned to look at a man and show on my face what I knew he wanted to see. That didn't mean that's what I was thinking. Most of the time I was thinking "How much longer do I need to be a whore for this man before he sees the special woman he has?" The problem with this was something he never saw until it was over. When I had enough of him and sadly, something I never saw in myself at all.

I was always told you have to love your self for someone to love you. Now I understand. If he didn't have something I wanted, trust me I would get tired of him. I became selfish in that way. You see, I wasn't always the one dropped in the relationship, but the breakup hurt just the same for me. Although I would not treat him badly, I would forget about him. I like to think I wasn't that cold but reality is, I was. I learned to use what I did well to hold on to a man I didn't even want. What I longed for with all my heart was a real relationship with a good man that just loved me. But instead, I continued to do what I knew, nothing ever got better. As the saying goes, "If you keep doing the same thing you will get the same results". I continued to deal with the same type of man, the one that says they want a loving relationship but reality, they want a constant booty call. Oh sorry, I am putting myself in a category that is too high, what they wanted from me was a whore. I stepped out of my place for a moment there and gave myself to much credit for who I was to the men I was with. A man that wanted me to give sexually with no commitment was not going to do right by me at any stage of our relationship, I know this all too well. What's funny is I have heard this saying from father's to daughters and then these same fathers' do this to someone else's daughter. Then, they're frustrated and angry when some guy hurts their little girl. Did they ever think of the women they are hurting and the anger and frustration that father feels? Gentlemen, are you picking up what I am putting down? What comes around goes around. Problem is, when you have to learn a lesson through a love one, it's even more painful of a lesson to learn.

I felt like mentally I was just falling apart. I could have tried for the rest of my life and would have never been able to put myself back together. Things were so bad that I fell into a deep depression. Hating the mere fact that I was alive. I lost all hope, everything looked dark and grey to me. Even when things in my life were good, I couldn't see it. I found myself trying to hold on to the most undesirable men just so I wouldn't be alone. Thinking this will give me happiness, this has to, right? Seriously, I couldn't be happy even if I had billions to pay for it, even if only temporary happiness. Then I thought to myself death, yeah that has to be the most perfect peace.

My mother is one of nine children from my grandmother. Sad to say my mother is the only living sibling at this time. So I had been exposed to many funerals in my life. The one thing I always remembered was being comforted or hearing someone being comforted. The words were always the same, "It's alright now, she or he is at peace now. No more pain". This was always followed by a loving hug and smile, to help the grieving person cope with what was happening at the moment. I had been searching for peace for years and now I know how to get it. Yes, so simple how did I not know? I remember saying to God, being so low when I made my decision to die. I said "If you won't talk to me, if you won't tell me why I keep going through this, why am I not worthy to have a husband? Why I have to continue to go through this heart ache and this pain that I can't handle any longer. I can't handle this any more, if you won't talk to me here on earth that's ok because I'll come see you. I'll take my life and I will come see you and then we can talk because I can't keep on going through this. I can't continue to go from relationship to relationship and feeling this pain. This pain of worthlessness, this pain of hopelessness, this pain of not even being human any longer. I feel like I am a blow up sex doll so I am just dressed up pretty when he is ready to have sex with me and then throw me to the side until I am wanted again for the same activity, no love or feelings. When I am no longer wanted I become a piece of crap. All while I am just dyeing inside, I'm dyeing inside. I need you to stop this Jehovah, to fix this I'm dyeing!"

I'm going to fast forward to the worst and best day of my life, which was one in the same. I started the day, got up – got dress - ran for the bus. But this day, the difference was... I wanted death more than I ever wanted life. And I was determined to get it! My work day started and I knew in my heart I had no intention of seeing a tomorrow, in my mind the decision was made. In my heart I was excited, inside...smiling. This was the day I was finally going to be happy beyond my wildest dreams. I knew this was the truth because my mind kept telling me this was the only way. Peace! I will have peace, just pure peace. What I so desperately sought out was at my fingertips. No more pain, no more hurt, no more despair this was the answer to everything for me.

My plan was to get a gun, I fantasized about

this gun. I would cock the hammer of that gun and I could hear it, like sweet music almost a comforting soothing lullaby. I would smile savoring the moment. A friendly kiss from a passionate lover. Helping it reach my temple, an erotic experience. Pulling the trigger for a brief moment pure bliss. Complete peace, so sweet, this was a daily thought and nightly dream. I was so elated with the decision I made, but something in my head said, "What about your daughter?" This thought was a big buzz kill. Like way back in the day when I went to a house party, everyone's enjoying the music its always that one person that hits the record player and screws it up for the rest. You spend at least five minutes complaining how that fool killed your jam.

I fought with my thoughts, "She's grown" I thought and her aunts will take care of her. I don't need to worry about her, I did my job now it's time for me and this is what I want. That fighting thought in my head said one word to me, SELFISH. As much as I wanted this, death in my mind was life. Sounds strange, but this was my only chance at peace, so I thought. I needed to think of my daughter and how this would effect her life. How would she go on with this traumatic event? So not that I wanted to, I sought help and chose to voluntarily commit myself to a psych ward of a hospital. For three days, which was more than enough. When I went into the psych ward, at the beginning when I was being registered in, I was asked a few questions. Then asked if I felt safe, meaning if I went home would I try to kill myself. I could have easily lied and left that place. I would have only been lying to myself, but the truth was I didn't feel safe. All I needed to do was say I wasn't suicidal and recant all I had said before to the person admitting me before I even went through the doors that locked behind me. I don't remember being told that once I entered the next room I was unable to leave.

Upon entering this room, I was led to. I was told to take everything off except my panties. First thing in my mind was "Oh NO!!!" and I thought "how can I get out of here", this is now becoming a nightmare. There was a big guy guarding the door as well as several other guards. Now I was confident on taking down the smaller guards. Through tears and fear, I cased the joint and figured out how I could handle myself. I think I was watching too many action movies. But that big dude, no I wasn't taking him down. Although they say no, I was threatened and I felt threatened. Everything was loud in there, patients yelling and screaming. Guards and nurses laughing and joking, which I found to be extremely inappropriate. Some of the most heartless people! They all needed to be retrained not a one with compassion. I remember changing my clothes, in the bathroom as I was demanded to do and then placed in a room. I was already depressed and suicidal but now I was stressed and scared on top of it.

The room was cement walls and floors, the TV was build in the wall and the staff had to control it for you. On a make shift platform, laid a mattress about two inches thick covered with a pliable plastic. I sat crouched in a corner, like a caged animal. My heart racing wondering to myself "What have I done? Why didn't I leave when I had the chance?" It was then a therapist came into the room to assist me. She was very nice, I remember her asking me if it was ok for her to sit with me on the floor. I stated to her that she did not have to sit on the floor, she was welcomed to sit on the bed. But she insisted on sitting with me on the floor. I agreed, she gave me a warm smile and copped a squat, as the saying goes.

We talked for about two hours, she was the very first person God brought to me. I told her how mean I was treated upon arrival, she could see how scared and upset I was. She spoke to me about God, calling Him by name. Asking me if I was offended or if she was crossing any lines. Honestly, I was so happy she was speaking to me about God and calling Him by name. I started to feel a little more at ease, not as an afraid caged animal, but more like a human. She stated I looked better and asked me to sit on the bed. I agreed and listened to what she said. I was feeling a little better. Now the conversation switched to the one question we both needed to know before we could move forward. "Are you feeling safe? Will you be ok if I release you to go home?" I looked at her and again I had the opportunity to lie and go home. But instead I said "No", that was the answer that came from my lips. "I can't promise you I will be safe, I still want to die. If I had lied, I believe I would have ended up worse then I was at that moment. And maybe just maybe I now wanted to live.

At that point it was explained to me that I would be moved to a different hospital to start treatment. She apologized for the way I was treated and gave me a great big hug then left the room. A new shift of guards came in, she explained what happen and asked if they could be a little kinder. I felt God sent me a protector. I stayed knowing I needed help and before I got to a point to were I didn't feel I could return from. I was made to think of the reason why I thought I was there, which opened up several doors and memories that I long thought I was over. It's amazing what the mind can block and lock away from your current thoughts, how it protects you from emotional pain. How God protects you, until He knows you're ready to face it.

I started having flash backs to the point it was as if I was there. I could see people as if they were standing in front of me. Smelling the scent of men that made my skin crawl, feel their hands on my body and taste things about them that I never want to ever think about again. I thought I was going insane. I wrapped my arms around myself, rocked my body back and forth crying. A very nice guard came into my room and gave me a blanket, I think he mistook my crying for shivering. Another guard came in and brought me some food I declined but he was kindly insistent, stating you must be hungry please eat a little then he smiled. Such nice jesters from both of them, showing me a light in this dark place.

Later the same evening I was transported to another hospital. I remember being so nervous upon arriving, again general staff really need to be retrained in the skills of compassion. As I was registering in the hospital, not yet entering the psych ward. The first day there I woke after a hard time sleeping, throughout the night bed checks are conducted. I needed to go to the bathroom so I went to the nurse's station to inquire where it was. The hallways where full of patients needing something. Loud talking some a little off the wall. Some completely depressed almost catatonic. Some just talked and talked and talked there was no silence no peace. The nurse so kindly states something on the lines of "honey all the rooms have a bathroom, it's located behind the door you walked out of". At that moment I completely broke down. The only other time I cried since this horrible event took place was when I initially came in to the hospital. Other than that I was able to keep myself under control, in all honesty it was because I was watching my own back. I made a conscious decision to fully trust no one. I went back to the room the nurse closely in tow, and sat on my bed. Still hysterically crying, unable to catch my breath tears soaking my face. Once I was able to catch my breath and calm down the nurse asked me if I was alright and why did I get so upset. I know she wanted to say over nothing but she was kind enough not to. She looked genuinely concerned for me. Really feeling the need to know why so she could help me, perhaps give me that stored up bit of advise she had been dyeing to administer for a long time. You know that savvy piece of advise that turns your life completely around. That's not what I got, however what I got was a kind conversation.

I explained to her I felt like a fool by being there. And she explained to me that anyone could be in this situation even herself she was not above getting completely overwhelmed. I have to say that helped to know I was not alone. I wouldn't want anyone to share in this misery but least I knew I wasn't alone in this. She became the second person that brought God to me. Although she did not say His name, I knew it was He she spoke of. Just the same, I felt comfort.

Sitting in that room alone, bars on the windows, conversations in the halls. The hustle and bustle of the day so different from my normal day. Then I thought "Will this be my normal day? What did I do to myself? Why didn't I just go home when I had the chance?" In my head was you need help, spiritual help.

I figured I was just losing it, but these words were not mine. I would ask a question and get an answer, but not my answer. That happened both times when I was asked if I were safe. No, really wasn't my answer I just figured it was because I said it. As I sat on my bed I had a vision, like a daydream. When I'm woke but these thoughts are not under my control. Most times they're random thoughts, but not this time it was very clear.

It started this way, two men came to me, not recognizing either one. One handed me a glass heart. This man handed me this heart promising me that I would be safe, promising that all would be well. This man handed me that heart with an evil smile on his face asking me to trust him. Asking me to believe in him he handed me this heart with what I thought was in all sincerity. As I reached out to take this heart, he promised that I would always be safe. This man promised me the world assuring me that it was his to offer. The heart broke and the man just looked and smiled a smile that was almost chilling not warm at all. Now the heart fell and broke in big pieces and I looked I was panic stricken I reached down and put those pieces together with my tears part of my soul and my belief, I was able to put that glass heart back together. I thought to myself "I got this. I'm ok." Now, you see when the heart was broken the man wasn't around, at least not to help. But he was at the beginning when he made the promises. Promises, that didn't last. That same heart fell again and when it broke the second time the pieces where smaller. The same man shot over the same cold chilling smile and this time some of his teeth showed and his teeth were white, white, white. Not normal, very odd but I couldn't place my finger on what was wrong. I again reached down because the pieces were big enough to put back together with my soul and my tears and my belief. Again this man caused the heart for a third time, he handed me to fall and break. However, the difference this time is when I reached down to pick these pieces up although the pieces were big enough to try but so small, I didn't know how I could possibly get those pieces back together. When I reached down to put those pieces back together, the man shot me a cold eerie smile as he crushed the remaining pieces under his foot. The man crushed them, more like pulverized those pieces to powder. Now at this point, I am feeling completely overwhelmed and completely dishearten that these pieces can't be put back together. The man looked at me, laugh and said, "Why would you think I would give you something? Who do you think you are? And why would you think you would be worthy to receive any thing from me?" The man called me a fool, he belittled and berated me and he told me that I belonged to him. I responded by saying, "How could I belong to you? I don't even know you!" The man responded by saying "Of course you do Tara, the man called me by name. The man went on to say you have been doing my bidding for years." The man smiled as he revisited my rape he brought the memories back so vividly I could feel his touch and smell his scent. "So sweet, so pure, so young", he almost purred these words in my ear. My stomach turned fear took over my complete body. Now I know who he is. Just as I could no longer stand him, just as I was about to give up and agree to belong to him. The room became light to were I could see the second man He stepped forward bent down and scooped up my pulverized heart. He put it in a glass and added water. Then He look at me and handed me the glass to drink, I was reluctant. The only question he asked me was, "Do you have faith?" I nodded my head took the glass and drank. I could feel my broken heart being restored, all the pieces finding their perfect place, A feeling of wholeness and completeness from the inside.

I realized there was a choice I needed to make. God spoke to me and reassured me of his love for me. I didn't believe He was talking to me at first. My thinking was my mind was playing tricks on me. It made no sense for God to want to talk to a worthless, nobody like me. As time went on, people started talking to me for whatever reason. God was mentioned for one thing or another. I was told to seek a higher power. I was told I looked as if I was a spiritual person and I should build on that. It's amazing just how God uses people.

Then it dawned on me, God is talking to me! And my second thought was "And I look like this?" You see, I was brought up to believe that you came to the Lord in your Sunday best and on Sunday. I wasn't fit to be in the presence of Jehovah God, my clothes, hair or my mental standing. I can't do this, not now. To be in God's presence I would need my dress, shoes and purse to match. And for the older ladies, which I am now a hat and you had to know how to wear it. I stood in a hospital gown open in the back, hospital pants no bra, security took it from me. How could I possibly stand before God? How could I let God see me? Then I thought, God isn't like a man that has no problem being with you when you are at your best. You know when your hair is done, clothes are beautiful, nails laid, the time you know you look your very best. That is when some men, not all, love you. God however, loves you at your worst as well as your best and every possible thing in between. God will be there for you to take you out of your worst and gently guide you to the best you can be. And that's not all, God continues to give you more. God's blessings never cease, God is loving and giving, I became a captivated audience. I sang out to the Lord in the voice that He gave me, because I had none of my own. The world, the enemy took that voice, that song away long ago.

Now I have a permanent song in my heart because of Him. God had my attention and I knew who He was just by the blessings He brought to me in that horrible place. The third day I was in the hospital, God showed me the path I was to walk on. This was not something I was told by God but shown to me by God in a vision. I was standing at the barred window in my room, in the hospital when God brought this vision to me.

An ordinary path you would see in the forest. Trees that seem to almost touch the sky lined up on either side of the path. Where I was standing on the path was dreary, but up ahead was bright. Now, I could see the path for miles in front of me. After that it got a little fuzzy. At one point on the path, was a fork. However, not showing me as two different paths but another path merging with mine. God held out His hand for me to hold. The ground was firm under my feet when I held His hand, but when I let go I fell down. I could feel my body fall like I was falling down a hole. I started to panic but then God put out His hand to me. I took His hand and instantly, was back on firm ground. God told me that this was my path. As God pointed to the ground He explained to me that my path will be like the pebbles and rocks on the ground. There will be pebbles that I can kick to the side, rocks that I can move, rocks that I will need to walk around and boulders that I will need to climb over. God said that as time went on and WE walked this path together, the path would be smoother. While I was in college in 1995 I wrote a paper on what I thought peace was, not fully understanding what I was writing. Now I see this was a part of the path God was showing me. I wrote: In the back of my mind, there is a place I call my own. As I sit and day dream, I in vision a large walnut double door with golden rings that hang as door knobs. As I pull open the door and step through the imaginary door way, I see the most beautiful sight ever seen by human eyes, rays of sunlight warming my toasty brown skin. I see a blanket of green grass hugging the ground beneath my bare feet. Grass greener than a forest green crayon and tall trees as if they were ladders to God. As I sit under the cool shady branches of a large tree, my back against the trunk, gazing up into the intoxicating blue sky. Sitting and dreaming of better days, as I run the tips of my fingers softly across the blades of grass that seem to cushion my body like a soft chair. Looking to my left, I see a pond with small fish, golden streaks dancing ever so smoothly through them. Although this is not a real place for you, it is certainly real for me in my mind! I'm able to imagine a place I know that will never come to ruin. God spoke to me in 1995 but it's only now I understand.

My heart became so peaceful as I stood on that path just holding God's hand for a long time. Not that I was afraid to let go, I didn't want to let go. That was the most inner peace I have ever experienced. God showed me I was worthy, that I could give and receive love. That my life was worth living, my life was going to change for the better because He had a plan for me. Now, did I know exactly what that meant? No, but at least now I had hope, a spring in my step, light at the end of the tunnel and finally a new song in my heart. This was the day I began my personal devotion to God.

~Presentation~

I was to busy cleaning up the outside while the inside was a hot mess. Sometimes I would pass by houses that were beautiful on the outside and wondered how do they look on the inside? Is this just a show so everyone assumes that all is just as beautiful inside as outside? For me I would cringe when my sister would bring me home. Seeing all the stuff on my lawn I was embarrassed almost to tears but I knew what others didn't. The inside was nice, neat, warm and inviting.

For so many years I worked on the outside thinking I needed to empress the on-looker. But reality I needed to work on what was more important, the inside. I made a bad mistake in my past of doing this same thing with myself. Concerned more of the dresses I would wear and shoes to match and OH! The shoes I have. The only thing this did was bring me misery. Because this is the way of the world, not a lot of real substance, just looking good.

I learned God would fill me, starting from the inside. Showing me how to love, give and share. Changing my mind from the old superficial ways to the new spiritual ways. Molding me into the person that I truly am and what I want to present to the world. I was so busy fixing what I thought was needed on the outside, I neglected the grave needs on the inside. When I stopped, reassessed and focused on the inside, God blessed the outside. When I stopped and gave all to God, He provided all. Every time I thought I needed something He already had it for me

<u>Matthew 6:8 states, 8-Do not be like them, for your Father knows what you need before you ask him.</u>

This is a process in my mind, heart and soul. I had to allow God to renew me.

Years ago when I was still a teenager I had just enlisted in the air force. I was in the reserve and this would be my first weekend serving. I made a huge mistake and I was devastated. Wanting to just give up, I was told it wasn't a big deal but I couldn't let it go. I remember one of the sergeants made this analogy. She said "Tara, what if you were walking down the street and you stumbled and tripped would you just stand there waiting for the laugher of the people that saw you to die down before you moved on? Or better yet, same street but instead of stumbling you fall. Flat on your face and scrap your knees on top of it. Then the people that saw you are laughing so hard they are in tears. So this is now adding insult to injury. What are you going to do? Are you going to lay there and refuse to get up thinking it will go away faster? Or are you going to get up shake it off and move on with you head held high knowing you did your best in that situation?" When she said that all I could think was "What !?!" and "Why do I care about tripping or falling?" It was my level of maturity at that time. I didn't get it, but I do now. There are times I feel I stumble and I am not doing as much as I feel I should for God. This too is a level of maturity to understand God forgives and I must repent and accept that forgiveness from Him. Also at times from myself to move on and continue serving God. Sometimes I doubt and question what I know is from God. But then I remember what is stated in the bible in:

Proverbs 24: 16 16-for the righteous falls seven times and rises again, but the wicked stumble in times of calamity

This brings comfort to me, not to make a habit of stumbling or falling, but knowing God will be there when I do.

4. stumble

~Hot mess~

I created a person that was completely not me, but I thought that person was me. You see, God is now revealing everything to me and I mean everything. When It comes to my life and my ways, God is pin pointing it all. I don't want to say my faults but He's just showing me who I was and how that is not who He meant me to be. I feel like I was covered from head to toe with Band Aids. I remember the saying when I was young, "Rip them off fast so they won't hurt as much." Well, I was still afraid to rip them off. Even though it's fast because pain is still attached to them. I feel like with every revelation I get, one of those Band Aids ripped off. But it's not like a slap in the face, it doesn't hurt like that. It's more like a firm tap on the hand, as if God is saying "Do you understand what I am saying? Do you understand what you were doing in the past was wrong? Do you see where you should be now?" More like a firm loving reminder, it doesn't feel like excruciating pain at all. I get a revelation, God will send me a revelation and I think to myself "Wow, I can't even dispute that. I did it!" I kind of just smile and sometimes I kind of giggle because I am trying to mask the shame of things I have done. I think to myself "Tara you were wrong, you were so wrong, you did wrong." Now God is correcting me and I feel better. I see the lessons are making me stronger and closer to God and His will, for a real relationship that I have always wanted. I have been begging God for that for years but I did not go forth for that to happen. God was always there and ready for me but I spent too much time rejecting Him and then blaming Him for not being close. But then I think, "How can I have that (relationship) if I'm not together within myself."

Then I thought, that is why I went to God because I wasn't together and I needed Him. See, you have to understand I looked very nice on the outside for my age. On the outside I could work a nice dress, shoes, hair, nails and such. But it seemed to be my only "claim to fame" as the saying goes. I looked good but on the inside, I was a hot mess. I was horrible, I created a facade of a person that wasn't really me. Through heartache, excuse, pain, worry, anxiousness, sorrow, disappointment, fear and insecurities, I created this person that had this tough exterior but was a complete mess on the inside. Allow me to help you understand, if my door bell rang and I did not know or did not expect anyone my heart would jump. I would be so anxious, on the outside you wouldn't see it but on the inside I was losing my mind. If something wasn't working temporarily in my house I would be unrealistically upset about it and again, it would be on the inside. I would become so damaged, if someone spoke to me I did not really want to speak back or didn't know what to say. On the outside I spoke said "Hi" but on the inside, concerned about what I said, thinking I have to avoid this person. Oh my goodness the door bell rang; oh my goodness is something broke? Oh no! Now I am going to be bankrupted because this is going to cost me a fortune. If someone walked by on the street oh goodness what are they going to do. I was a hot mess on the inside God is showing me exactly what a hot mess means with those examples, because I would say I was a hot mess on the inside but I couldn't explain. I knew what I meant but I couldn't explain it. Everything upset me, everything worried me. Not just the common everyday things, but irrational things as well. Like, the door bell and the inability to interact with folks. I was stressed out about everything from, I needed a pair of shoes, Where was I going to get the money? I needed to get to work where's my bus pass. I needed to get to the bus stop am I going to get there on time? What am I going to do? How am I going to do it? How will things get done? How do I get here, how do I get there? I want a cup of coffee do I have the money? How are my bills? How is my life? I got to a point where I couldn't function. But when I handed all my worries, stress, sorrow, fear, anxiety all of my problems to God, the issues no longer existed. Even in sleep I was anxious. Now all that has ceased because I gave it all to Jehovah God. I trust Him completely to put my life in His hands and He is taking care of all of those worries. Now, does it take time? Yes! Did it take time for me to grow so I could give all my worries to God? Yes! Will I never make another mistake now that I put my life in God's hands accepting Jesus as my Lord and Savior? No. I will make daily mistakes we all do, but what is so wonderful about Jehovah God is that He will always be there for me to give me that next chance. I have comfort in the words of:

1Peter 5:6-7 and Ephesians 1:7. 1 Peter 5: 6-7
6-Humble yourselves, therefore, under the mighty hand of God so that at the proper time he may exalt you, 7-casting all your anxieties on him, because he cares for you

Ephesians 1: 7   7-In him we have redemption through his blood, the forgiveness of our trespasses, according to the riches of his grace

~Mr. Right~

I know I've mentioned before that I was raped at age 17 and I thought that I dealt with it. But instead, I just pushed it down deep inside of me and didn't deal with the pain and confusion that rape caused. I thought I was dating men that looked like the man that raped me to find some sort of acceptance. Almost like I was trying to get some sort of validation from these other men because of what this first man stole/robbed from me. I felt worthless and for some strange reason, I thought that these other men would give me that sense of self worth back, it doesn't work that way.

Not all the men I've dated were like this but, in a since they were because of what they all had in common. It was a sense of non-caring and aggressiveness. Once they got what they wanted, they didn't care anymore. I didn't matter and I no longer cared. In my mind, I wasn't human anymore I was a place for them to put their penis and nothing more. But I allowed this and I seem to seek this out because of my own insecurities. Not knowing my self-worth, I spent my adult life just "winging it". What I mean by that is, I just let the important things in my life just happen. I settled for anything. I did not put effort into it or plan it, I figured if that is all I got, then that's all I deserved. I winged my whole life until now, from my house, which I didn't necessarily want. But I took it because of the crumbs that came my way. After a while, no real thought at all was put into any relationship of mine. I single that out because in the chapter this is what I am talking about. A combination of no self worth and not really caring. So why am I so shocked when it doesn't work? With my relationships, with my job. Everything, from the curtains that were hanging on my windows, to the paint that I chose on my walls, to the the clothes that I wear. Even with my shoes, a lot of the shoes that I have I don't want them. They were cheap enough or they just happen to be there and I just took them because I wanted something at the time. And whatever ones

I bought were, better than not having anything at all. I winged everything in my life however, now with God I'm finding that I'm selective about everything.

Now I'm working on making the things that I winged in the past work. Now like my house, doing things to make it a home that I want. Because I didn't take the time to really choose the home that I wanted, I'm trying to make this house my home. God is making that happen. I'm selective when I buy clothes, shoes and things I'm just more selective all around. I have a job a good job I was blessed to have the job that I have and I am making this job the best that I can now. It's not my dream job but I am making it my dream job. This is not my dream house but I am making it my dream house. I am finding that I am not so quick to just accept things, now I have standards and I want things certain ways. I'm just not letting life fall on me anymore. I'm really taking the time to consult with God and see what is His will and what is best for me according to

His will. These are the things that are going to make me happy and not things I have to figure out how it's going to make me happy in the future.

When I look back on most of the relationships I was in, I didn't care much for. One time I remember, going to an eatery with a man. He was so rude to the waiter and by the time the food was brought to us, I looked very hard to make sure no spit was in it. The new me would have been polite and left that situation, not only physically but mentally. The old me stayed because I thought he was better than I could ever get. Why? sadly because he had. But really BIG DEAL!! I have and I like what I have. And I was no slob as well, beautiful, intelligent, sexy, well spoken, upbeat, just a lovely person. But I did not see that, so I settled for far less than I should have. I didn't have enough within me to demand more, to want more, to care about more, to know my value for more.

I figured because I was raped that sex wasn't

important. Sex was just a function it was something that you did like urinating or drinking an ice cold glass of water on a hot summer day. Sex was a function to me. So I assumed I knew what you're here for. I know you're here to have sex, let's do what we got to do and move on. But that just made things worse because I feel worse about myself for having sex. Somewhere along the way, I stopped looking for Mr. Right and settled for Mr. Right now, Mr. Today and Mr. You will do. It didn't help the situation at all because what I wanted the most, what I craved for the most and what I needed the most was even further away from me.

News flash!!! I cried and wondered about feeling sorry for myself, being the victim. Asking God how could these men do this to me. After praying, I stayed quiet and listened. God revealed what was truly in my heart. After being raped, I was looking for a man to validate me. And yes, most of them looked a lot like the man that raped me. I thought I wanted one of them to tell me he loved me and I wasn't trash. In turn, that's not what I was looking for I was looking for that type of man to hurt and destroy his heart, to be in control. Then and only then I felt I would regain what I had lost. It was all about a sick, twisted, revenge not validation. This was so hard for me to except. However, I know it rings truth. At some point in my life, I had to ask myself this question. "What is he doing for me? Why is he here? He had me thinking he'd move the mountains, but in reality he hasn't even push a pebble." In other words, I allowed him to have me believe more than what he was really doing.

Say my man brings me flowers, I say "Oh my goodness! This is so lovely my, man brought me some wildflowers." To me, this is so nice and thoughtful. He stopped off at the store or a vendor and thought of me. Then I find out no, he didn't stop at a store or vendor, where he stopped was the neighbors yard and snatched them as he walked through. No longer thoughtful. I slowly started to see that if his only claim to fame is putting it down in the bedroom, then he wasn't the one for me. My soul was lost, not caring about anything, so painful. The hardest part for me once I surrendered myself to God was to wait for God's guidance. To wait for God to fix the wrong I was dealing with outside but especially within me. To provide the thing I desire. But the bible tells me to be still.

<u>In Psalms 37:7 7-Be still before the Lord and wait patiently for him; fret not yourself over the one who prospers in his way, over the man who carries out evil devices!</u>

Through all my many mistakes, that I could have avoided if I had listened to God, I realized because of God, waiting is always best. God knows what you need, as stated in:

<u>Matthew 6: 8 8-Do not be like them, for your Father knows what you need before you ask him</u>

as well as not standing on your own knowledge as stated in:

Proverbs 3: 5 5-Trust in the Lord with all your heart, and do not lean on your own understanding.

~My Condition~

Sunday church service, August of 2014. I wasn't feeling my very best this day. I posted on my Facebook page that morning before leaving for church, "God's blessings and happiness comes when you meet Him at least half way... And from my calculations that halfway point for me today is church... I pray He is happy with me, because today was hard". Service started, Pastora Cindy began praise and worship, I looked to my right and there sat a couple, to the left another couple. Behind me, a man had his arm around his wife. And directly in front of me, which was the straw that broke the camels back, not only a couple but the whole family. I became so upset I left the service forgetting to take my bag, bible or notepad.

Crying, I walked outside the church around the corner to the back of the church when I realized I did not have my keys. In complete despair, I fell down on the curb and cried. A sister from the congregation that met before ours stopped to see if I was ok, answering that I was ok, she blessed me and drove away, I wasn't ok. So I walked back to the front stairs of the church.

Elder Jennifer came out to offer me a bottle of water, a hug and a kind word, my selfishness rejected her. The following Thursday I was so upset and crying, on my way to leave church. Pastora Cindy stopped me, trying to help and comfort me, she too was rejected by me. Elder Manuel was the next to try to comfort me. I shot him a look like as if to say, "Don't bother me!" and just plain "Leave me alone!" Again my foolishness and ignorance. The following Sunday Pastor Eliezer approached me, he was more stern in his ways, not allowing me to walk away.

He stated one thing to me, more like a question which made a world of difference in my life. It was a statement that was said to me in the past by a woman I once worked with. I don't remember her name, something common like Barbara or Sue or Mary, however she was no common woman. I remember her being so kind and truly caring. Every holiday she would give everyone a gift. She had at least four grandchildren and managed to bring each one of them on vacation. I thought this was amazing seeing that I was in a position at that time where me and my daughter were barely eating. I had nothing and convinced myself that I never would.

My co worker sat me down and explained when she was my age she too had nothing. It was her and her husband and they could hardly provide food in the house. She told me a story of not even having a decent pair of shoes when she was pregnant with one of her children, having to walk in the snow with the cold and the wet getting to her feet. She had nothing then, but people helped her and now she can't repay the people that helped her but she can do for others. I remember her lovingly explaining to me the only way I would stay in that condition of having nothing would be because I choose to stay there. Because I think and believe I should be stuck there. This brings me back to Pastor Eliezer, he asked me if I wanted to stay in the condition that I was in? Unlike the co worker, she was cut and dry, Pastor's question was a little tricky. "No, I don't but what do I do about it?" was my reply. Pastor Eliezer said that I needed to open up when things bothered me, regardless of what it is. I remember my co worker telling me to work hard and I would succeed. What I need was a relationship with God which would definitely take work. All relationships take work so why would this be any different. I needed to open up to Him and the people He sends to me. Pastor Eliezer helped me to understand that whatever was bothering me, I needed to give those worries to God. To trust in God and allow Him to heal the pain of my past so I could change my thought patterns. And thus, no longer would I be stuck in the condition I was in. That would be hard for me, because as my daughter so nicely put it "Ma, you're very introverted". It's amazing to me how God took this person and her words from my past intertwined with words from my Pastor in my present to make a better future for me. I understand and I am thankful to God. One more piece of the future God intended for me to live and grow in.

~Side Chick~

"Why am I being treated like the side chick?" was the question I asked myself. My attitude was, I don't want to be the side chick. There are so many women that wanted to be the side chick for one reason or another. So why treat me that way if I am giving all of me and I want something real.

Because that is how I was showing myself. One thing I never did was hide how I truly felt and what I really wanted in a relationship, love, respect, and to be cherished. Being unable to feel that way for myself is what limited someone else to feel that way for me.

One day I was waiting at the bus station, it was a cold day and I kind of zoned out. Just thinking of getting home and resting. It had been a long day and I wasn't feeling too well. I noticed a young girl in line to get on one of the buses. I should say we all noticed her, she was talking to her friend, swearing and cussing, sounding completely unladylike and just plain disgusting. It was sad that she did not have enough respect for herself to show herself better than that. Shaking my head and thinking to myself she really showed herself so bad to all of us. The thing is who are we in her life? Nobody! But, she didn't care and or didn't seem to know better. I think the worst of it was, the on-lookers didn't seem to care. The looks on their faces told me they had already counted her out as a productive part of society. She was seen as the norm, she couldn't do better so why should they waste their time or expression of disappointment on her.

As I was standing there a man walked up to me and made a comment on how that young lady was speaking. The guy's point was, "When ladies like her," as he said "speak that way, men look at them very different." We spoke on that for a few moments and then that conversation became a gateway to his opinion on how women show themselves and how men perceive them. I wasn't too interested in the conversation at first but this topic peaked my interest.

The man began by explaining to me that he started to talk to a girl and his original interest was high, meaning he was interested in dating her for the purpose of a relationship. "Ok," I said to myself "that's nice, this is a stand up guy. Then he said that the girl stated that she was only looking for a casual type of thing. This man continued by saying at this point, his interest was lowered. And again my thought was, "Ok, this is a stand up guy. He is not looking for that and he will tell her." NO! He didn't. As he continued to speak on the topic I came to realize he had an opportunity and instead of being that up standing guy. He did as many do, take advantage, use and then blame her. Then I thought to myself, "Tara, you are taking the position of a victim. Boohoo Tara the big bad men in this world just use good women. They just seek out women they can do wrong and if you complain enough to the world, the world will feel bad. Snap out of if Tara, wake up!" So quickly I slid back to the victim roll. I realized from this man, this unsolicited conversation, that we as women have more control in a relationship then men.

You will be a victim if you allow yourself to be a victim. Don't count on a man to be the up standing person you need him to be. Instead, be the up standing woman God has made you to be! After that moment, I pulled my head out of my, "you know what". I posed a question to myself, If this man was looking for something more or serious and she was a person, he could see to be more or serious with then why not ask what she really meant by casual. Because we don't always know what we want or what we need.

Matthew 6:8 states: 8-Do not be like them, for your Father knows what you need before you ask him.

We should all know young or old there is a possibility that this person may not know exactly what they want but if you walk into it knowing what you want, your conscience should make sure that you are both on the same page. Not to belittle yourself and give her little respect. If what she said is what she meant, why not just explain he was interested in more and let that go. I think that would be the right thing to do. But is that always going to happen? No, definitely not saying there's no stand up guys out there. Just saying God gives us the strength to stand up for ourselves to make decisions through His teachings to do what is right. By the end of this conversation with this man, I realized what I had been doing was wrong. I realized why I had not met my Mr. Right and why my heart was constantly being broken. There was a reason why a conversation was struck up between myself and this man, in fact a blessing. God knew I needed answers to my questions regarding men/relationships. God knew this man was the impartial view I needed to move on, see what I did, stop beating myself up and heal. Because until I heal, God can't introduce me to the man He prepared for me.

THE GLORY OF GOD REVEALED!

5. God

~Depression~

I remember loving depression, just loving it! Depression was my boyfriend, my lover and my friend. Depression was my comfort, that's the emotion I was most comfortable with. I remember going home on a Friday after work, and being in my room until Monday morning because depression had a hold on me. And I was okay with it. It was bad enough the enemy had me low, low wasn't enough for the enemy he needed me low low and I welcomed it. I was sickly in love with my depression. It was the only emotion that was consistent in my life. I held it and cuddled it like a baby, depression was my baby. Why? Because depression made so many excuses why I didn't do what I needed to do. Depression lied for me, I really believed my depression protected me.

I had hopes and dreams that I never completed because of depression, this emotion allowed me to be a victim and gain sympathy with others. Again, allowing me not to take responsibility. If I cried on the shoulder of the right person, I no longer had to do for myself. That only lasts for so long. That was my excuse, my reason. Well, I'm so depressed I can't do this. I'm so depressed I can't do that. Then for a brief time period, I started to take all these depression pills and all that did was make me more depressed. Those pills allowed me to crawl right in the belly of depression, it felt better than before. However, the pills made me focus better but slower, I started to feel this overwhelming feeling of being trapped in my own head. My hopes, dreams and the small amount of zest I had for life started to slip through my fingers. I became a walking zombie, I was only functioning. Depression was eating at my very soul and stripped me of my feelings.

The only time I felt some sort of feelings was

when I was with someone I loosely called a boyfriend. The physical time together was the only time I could feel any emotions close to joy or happiness. But even with all that negativity, depression was still my best friend. When God took all that away from me, he freed me from depression and freed me from feeling that the only happiness was to be with someone. Jehovah taught me that He was enough, as in:

<u>2 Corinthians 12: 9. 9-But he said to me, "My grace is sufficient for you, for my power is made perfect in weakness." Therefore I will boast all the more gladly of my weaknesses, so that the power of Christ may rest upon me.</u>

There was a moment, just a slight moment I missed my friend because the depression was ingrained in me for most of my life. However, it was gone, no longer my friend, boyfriend or lover. No longer looking for depression to comfort me. I knew it, I felt it I know the difference between myself and being depressed.

Psalm 43:5 states: 5-Why are you cast down, O my soul, and why are you in turmoil within me? Hope in God; for I shall again praise him, my salvation and my God.

God freed me, I still need to read and apply God's word for my mind frame to change. To be able to not only realize but to accept the blessings that God has given me. James 1:22-24 tells me:

22-But be doers of the word, and not hearers only, deceiving yourselves. 23- For if anyone is a hearer of the word and not a doer, he is like a man who looks intently at his natural face in a mirror. 24- For he looks at himself and goes way and at once forgets what he was like.

~Packages~

You know the saying; "A pretty package doesn't always mean there is a good gift inside." I remember saying to myself that I wanted a man of a certain race, certain background, certain financial stability, certain hobbies and involves himself in certain activities. I wanted a certain type of man but I was too busy worrying about the outside of a man. As well as only worrying about the outside of me. I will say I was a pretty package outside, but very little beauty on the inside. I have to be fair, when I think about it, what was I really bringing to the possible relationship? The part everyone could see that's a pretty package however once I got to know that person, the package in a lot of cases was no longer pretty.

I could see just how wrong I was in the way I looked for someone and how I was displaying myself. Realizing the gift inside was pretty much worthless, no kindness, caring, compassion and or mercy. Nothing there to make me feel special to him, or him to me. So it was really a waste of time. Sometimes I picked a prettier package because I thought the gift was of greater value. But reality is I didn't know if I was picking the correct person for me or I for him. Choosing someone in the superficial way, in the end result, is a crapshoot.

Remembering the last date I had, before God entered my life in 2014. I was wearing a Black form fitting dress, with a crinkly type texture and a little shine. Bellow the knee, low cut with a stand up collar. I was feeling sexy and alluring, eyes were on me. Men wanting, women envying, when I think back, some women wanting as well. Shoes and purse on point, couldn't tell me nothing. I knew it was all about me this night. Who am I kidding, every time I wore this outfit it was all about me. So of course I would wear it tonight I really wanted to impress him. Almost gave up, one more chance I'll take just one more. Late, he's late is he really going to show up I wonder? Not feeling so confident anymore, insecurities seeping in. Don't want any one to see what I feel. Arrogance sets in to hide my feeling of worthlessness. Reached into my purse to call a cab to leave. Just at that very moment a text "I'm running late be there in 15". Regained a little of my outer confidence, ok there he is, I see him crossing the parking lot.

Wow! Nice looking! Eyes wide open, I didn't want to miss a thing on this man. He walked up to me and introduced himself, that voice, inside I was melting, I could listen to his voice forever. He opened the door and pulled out my chair, I can't remember the last time someone treated me like a lady. We talked and laughed, have a lot more than I would have ever thought in common. A song from the 80's comes on, wow we both knew it. His voice, that voice, his eyes dreamy but his smile was my favorite. Now it's getting late, he took me home, our attraction for each other is over whelming. So much happened it felt right then. As we parted all seemed great, until the next day, really not the next day exactly but the next week and a half later. Like a bomb, I have no idea what happened. I now felt worthless and used. Knowing this is at my own hand and I allowed this made it even worse. I started to see the dress in a different light as I saw myself as trash and cheap, I no longer wanted that attention. As I stupidly stripped that dress off me that night, feeling my soul stripped presently.

The enemy's gifts are always temporary and at a high cost. Through flowing tears, I picked up this dress preparing to destroy what I saw to be sinfully evil garbage, which simultaneously I felt about myself. I figured if I throw this dress away all the hurt and pain will be thrown away as well and I will be whole again. When out of nowhere I stopped, no understanding why I put the dress away. It wasn't until several months later, God explained to me there was nothing wrong with my dress. What God said I needed to do was upgrade it. What? Upgrade? What?!? He explained I needed to look at it with different eyes, not just sight but with vision. I wanted to believe God was talking really about the dress, but what He did was use the dress to make me look at myself. God allowed me to see I wasn't useless for anything other than dressing up and looking my best. To see myself with vision, not just by sight. I have substance and I shouldn't just see myself as window dressing. I need to see, look and want to develop the inside, upgrade not destroy.

I pulled out the dress I declared to be the dress of a whore and upgraded it to elegance. I am so grateful that God wasn't so quick to throw me away as I wanted to throw away the dress. God taught me about myself as well as what is truly important regarding relationships. What to look for and do more within myself. Choosing a man based on what type of qualities I would like in a spouse is more of a realistic way of choosing someone I may want to spend my life with. Galatians 5: 22-23 shows qualities I would like in the man I choose. Based on the fruits of the spirit as the Bible states:

22- But the fruit of the Spirit is love, joy, peace, patience, kindness, goodness, faithfulness, 23- gentleness, self- control; against such things there is no law.

I also want to be able to have these fruits of the spirit as well. Being a person that wants to have these qualities and looking for these qualities will provide a more secure relationship. And when I took the time to seriously think, I would receive what God intended a relationship, friendship and marriage to be. By applying and seeking someone as well that applies these fruits of the spirit, I will find a better person suited for me. Because their fruits are going to show me what kind of person they are in the respects of the fruits that are shown. As for the outside, that's the icing on the cake or the gravy on the mashed potatoes. But that's not the bulk or the most important qualities, those are the extras.

~Amusement Park~

When I first started going to church my first thought was "Yes, I want to serve God but I wanted a boyfriend, I don't want to be single." My mind frame stayed the same, I just wanted a good guy. I was still kind of dating when I first came to church. Now as time went on and it takes a little time because God has to soak into your mind. You have to realize that your mind frame has to change. As I applied God's word in my life, I no longer wanted a boyfriend I now wanted a husband. Which is great! However, my mind frame still needed a little more, in the sense that I wanted a husband but I wanted him so that I could have sex without feeling guilty. Without fornicating, technically I could have sex because he was my husband. I still needed a little more work on my thinking.

As time went on, I started realizing that mind frame was just a recipe for disaster. Nothing good would come of that. Because I'm still not choosing someone for the right reasons. Learning more about God's word and what God expects of me, I started realizing what I want is a man that puts God first! No negotiation on that, this is a requirement for me. The man I consider to be my husband MUST put God first because if he doesn't, I know he is not the man for me. I will instantly know this is not the man God has prepared to be my husband. I definitely want to have things in common with him. I want to be attracted to him you know, things like that are necessary as well.

I remember my thinking was, "He puts God first so the rest doesn't matter it will be okay because I will be married." Again, putting God first is a requirement. However, God made me realize that for a positive and successful marriage, compatibility is important as well. And I am a hard person to match someone up with. My interest is all over the map, from hobbies to activities and anything in between. God is the only one that could possibly handle that tall order of finding me a spouse. Because that man will be so important in my life, it is not as easy as I thought in the past. Thinking I would just find somebody and that will be the man I am with. Good or bad it doesn't matter because no marriage is perfect. The problem I found with that thinking is, if God wanted me to do something and my husband has an issue with it this will cause undue stress and pain in what should be a happy marriage. I want someone in my life that really loves me so I have trust in God because He is the only one that can provide that person for me. In Ecclesiastes 7: 12 I am reminded of how God protects me, the scripture states:

12-For the protection of wisdom is like the protection of money, and the advantage of knowledge is that wisdom preserves the life of him who has it.

God gives me the wisdom so better choices

can be made. Reminds me of when I was small and I would go to an amusement park. There was always a ride that I had my heart set on riding. But before I could get on it I had to be a certain height, weight or both. There it was a big card board sign in front of the ride with a picture showing just how tall you had to be. I remember being disappointed because year after year I wasn't tall enough. At the time I didn't see that it was for my own good, my own safety. As a child, I didn't see that I just wanted what I wanted. So when you think about that ride, you have to be a certain height. Because if you're not that height, you can get hurt on that ride and you become a liability to the amusement park. Things didn't really change as I grew up. I wanted what I wanted, not seeing that I wasn't ready and God was protecting me. From the pain and frustration of moving to fast in a relationship I wasn't ready for or wasn't meant for me. God knows when I am ready, as well as who is the right person for me my faith is with God on this.

By listening, I don't experience the pain of rejection I had in the past. I understand now that there is a certain set of requirements for someone to even begin to start talking to me in a serious manner. Which is dating leading to marriage. God's will, God's wants, God's word, and God's ways must come first! God is non-negotiable! My love for God will never allow me to accept anyone in my life that close to me if he does not share the same love for God. This requirement is not to hurt or make me feel lonely, it's to protect me, this is truly a blessing.

6. What I have learned

~Afro~

When I was about six or seven years of age, I remember in the 70s the Afro was a big hair style for African Americans. It was a natural type of hair style, and you used a pick to keep it rounded. My brother would always let me pick his hair. I too had an afro and when my Mom picked mine she would get way down to the scalp. So when I would pick my brother's hair I would start at the scalp like my Mom did. But when I would start he would say "No, Ouch!" My brother would flinch and say "No no Tara, pick from here", he was pointing at the top. "Just rake over-the-top." he would always say to me. I would say to him "And how do you get all the stuff underneath and make that nice and smooth like mommy does to mine?" And he would say "No just rake over the top", meaning just glide the pick over the top so it looks good, "and that's good enough." I know for a long time in my life that's what I did. I didn't take the time to really look at myself I didn't take the time to really get underneath and get to the problem. I just wanted to make sure the front or the outer part of me was really nice but, I didn't think about all the stuff that I neglected on the inside. In the bible,

Lamentations 3:40 states: 40-Let us test and examine our ways, and return to the LORD!

I realized that at some point the things that I choose to neglect on the inside would managed to cause me a lot of pain because I refused to look at myself. When I finally did take the time to straighten them out, I saw myself in a way I really didn't want to face. Why? Because I had to examine and test myself to return to the LORD. I made a habit of justifying my actions. Now I saw, not everything I was doing was right.

~Back in the day~

Back in the day we were not rich or well off. As matter-of-fact, I really didn't have everything I wanted. However, my mother made sure I had self-respect, self-worth and self-esteem due to her example. I have a huge amount of it now, but somewhere in between my mom's teachings and now regaining it, I lost so much of it. Yes! I was a hot mess. I was a single woman and a single parent and, sad to say, sometimes when you're single living in the ghetto the attitudes toward you are, you're easy. Also, you're willing to be with any man. But that's not really always the truth for every woman.

For me, I had so much more I wanted in a relationship. Knowing this I wanted much more but I didn't always get it. Just anyone shouldn't do, granite my standards weren't really high but they weren't really low either. Fast forward to just a mere eight months ago (6/2014) my standards had gone down so low that I didn't even recognize myself anymore. Now, granted I looked good on the outside but, I was so ugly and low on the inside that I had no more faith in myself. My faith should have been in God, not myself. That was a big mistake I made. I began going on dating websites, I ended up meeting nice men, men that had money. Something new for me because most I had dated up to that point did not. Moving forward, some really did and some didn't but they all played a good game. You would think a man with money has in some cases education, hence to obtain said money. In a lot of cases these men were worse then the men I knew I couldn't count on. I thought they were decent men but the fact is it doesn't matter whether a man is poor or rich or something in between, if they're not going to do right they're not going to do right. I thought and believed, someone more financially stable would be a better person for me. I thought he would be the person I needed in my life to make me better on the inside.

When a man spoke to me anyway he wanted

to, it's like I gave him a piece of my self-esteem, my self-worth and my self-respect. That's more important, more valuable than the piece of ass that he thinks he's going to get from me. Because my self-esteem, self-worth and self-respect was not tangible, not physical, not something you can hold in your hand. You can't taste it you can't touch it, you can't smell it and you can't see it. I wasn't sure just how to value it. Now I am not talking about the nice loving way I was spoken to by a man. I am speaking of when the conversation is not one of feeling up lifted and secure. When the conversation is abusive or boarder line abusive. My self-esteem, self-worth and self-respect is more important than the physical aspect, because every time a man spoke to me anyway he wanted, that was like giving him that much more of myself from the inside. At some point in a relationship, I would give him everything until I had nothing more to give. When I no longer had anything more to give, I no longer had a reason to care. However, the bible tells us this:

Ephesians 3:16-19 16-that according to the riches of His glory He may grant you to be strengthened with power through His Spirit in your inner being, 17-so that Christ may dwell in your hearts through faith—that you, being rooted and grounded in love, 18-may have strength to comprehend with all the saints what is the breadth and length and height and depth, 19-and to know the love of Christ that surpasses knowledge, that you may be filled with all the fullness of God

This scripture lets me know that it was then and still is currently, the fulfillment of God that will make me whole on the inside. Not someone on the outside, but God within me.

~Giving it away~

One night while laying in my bed, listening to music unwinding from the day, I was suddenly startled from a loud crashing type noise. I jumped up out of bed to see what was happening. I would have never thought in a million years it was in the apartment so I was looking out the window. I did not see anything but then I could hear someone in the living room. My closet door opened and shut then I knew he (I found out later it was a guy) was on my entertainment center and tried to steal the VCR. Going through my personal things, I felt terrified and violated. I thought, who could be in my apartment and what he or they would do because at this point I did not know if it was one or more in the apartment.

The fear levels rose, my heart in my throat. I ran to my daughter's room grabbed her out of bed and brought her in my room. I motioned for her to get under the desk and be still. I called the police, I was crying and scared out of my mind. The dispatcher informed me to stay locked in the room until the officer's arrived on seen. Once the officers came, we were able to assess the damages. One broken sliding glass door, one stolen wallet (which I now needed to replace and cancel all within it), one damaged VCR, one huge mess and lastly, one terrified and angry woman! After that everything was URGENT, canceling cards, making reports, cleaning up, fixing the sliding glass door and getting an alarm. I knew that fast was important to regain a sense of wholeness, to heal and to move forward in my life. I find that when the enemy steals from you all at once, people rally around you and help you to get back on your feet as quickly as possible.

When the enemy steals from you little by little. I see it more this way, kind of like when you're in a house and it's your dream house. Let me illustrate, I remember when I was a child and I would draw a house. Using my trusty crayons, the big ones that fit just perfectly in my little hands. The bright colors always made me happy, which I must say put me in the best mood to draw my dream house. I would draw a friendly house, so inviting to the on-looker of my master piece. Starting with a box and a triangle on the top. I always had a door that was so welcoming, bright in color. A red no, a green well, maybe a yellow. Yes, yellow! Others would make their doors black or brown but not me I wanted people to visit and a yellow door would do the trick. The windows, I always drew four panes of glass in my windows. Two windows in the front of the house and two in the back but you couldn't see them and one way up in the attic. Curtain's with polka dots, flowers or my favorite, butterflies. Last but not least, as the saying goes, a red brick chimney with a gray curly mark to show the smoke from the fire. I drew a chimney so I could imagine a nice warm inviting fireplace on the inside with a nice crackling fire blazing. This was my perfect place of pure happiness which is why it was in fact my dream house.

The house represents me how I saw myself. How comfortable I was once with myself. But now imagine this dream house is a reality. The window way up in the attic, the security latch is broken. You aren't aware of this but there is a thief that is. This thief has made it his business to watch your house, to see what way he can get in without you knowing. Now this thief comes in every day and steals one small thing. You think to yourself, "What happened to that picture frame? I placed it right here on the hallway table." Then you think "Well I am to busy to look and maybe it fell behind the table. I will look later I don't have time now." But then little by little this thief takes a small item from you daily. Instead of doing something, raising alerts we brush it off and make excuses. Thinking that's not big enough to stress about. To replace all the items the thief steals, is costly at the end.

That's the way the enemy took from me, believing as the world does, that my behavior is ok. However, I must admit much of what the enemy took I gave. How is that? By not trusting in God, not believing in God and not drawing close to God. The enemy took for many years from me. But then as time went on, he didn't have to take anymore. Because I got to a point where I lost a sense of myself. Once I started believing that I felt I had gone too far and I went to a level where God could not possibly want me or want to love me. I felt as if God abandoned me. When truth is, He didn't abandon me but in my mind, He did. That's when I started giving pieces of my soul to the enemy and I didn't even realize that's what I was doing. The enemy made me afraid to admit there was an issue and too embarrassed to speak on it. Too busy holding on to my pride, not wanting any one to see my flaws. I looked at it this way, if I showed my weaknesses than I would be like everyone else, not the person I set myself up for everyone to see. The outer appearance of having power, elegance and style. But the truth was knowing I had none of that, it was all a facade. After a while, he doesn't have to be a thief that comes in that attic window. Now the enemy came right to the front door and I was willing to open the door for him. That's what the enemy did to me, that's what he wants he wants to be able to come right into the front door and not even have to sneak into that top window. Because I allowed myself to get so low, I wasn't even willing to fight anymore, I became so broken, so low. My self-worth was low, my self-esteem was low, my spirit was low, my soul was low and my heart was low. So low it became black and brittle, I just didn't care anymore.

John 10: 10 helps me to stay hopeful, the scripture states:

<u>10-The thief comes only to steal and kill and destroy. I came that they may have life and have it abundantly</u>

The enemy is here to destroy and he does this in any way he can. God sent His son so through Him we may have life.

~Red Rover, Red Rover~

Remembering a childhood game, red rover red rover. The way it went, you would say "Red rover red rover send so-and-so over." Then so-and-so was whoever that kid you're calling. In this childhood game that kid is going to come running toward you. If my aging memory serves me correctly, there's a line of kids and they hold hands tight. You call "Red rover red rover send whoever it is over." The child comes running over and tries to break through the children holding hands, that's the goal of the game.

Now let me explain how I think the enemy is playing. With this game, you know that the kid is coming, it isn't a shock it isn't a surprise. You know that kid is coming, you called for that kid. So when the kid comes and hits your arms sometimes you're still not prepared. That first hit is always a surprise even though you know it's coming, even though you know what to look for, it still a surprise. So the first kid that comes barreling through is pretty much safe because if nothing else he caught you at the element of surprise, even though you knew.

When the second kid comes, the children in the line that are holding hands always tighten up a little more. They got their game faces on now and they're not going let anybody through. Now there's less and less kids that get through the barrier. Why? Because they know what's going to happen it's not just the thought of what's going to happen, they actually already experienced it. Which kids hits harder and the line has to tighten up. The ones that hit softer and the line can relax a little but still stay aware. Which makes it a little easier to deal with and that is what the enemy does. I knew he was coming and I knew what he was about. Knowing what he's about, I knew what I was to expect, but because it hasn't happened yet or it hasn't happened before I wasn't quite sure of the impact. But once it happened I, like the game, was prepared for the next time and believe me it will happen again. Because the enemy is a creature of habit. In 2 Corinthians 2:11 states this about the enemy

> *11-so that we would not be outwitted by Satan; for we are not ignorant of his designs*

So as long as I stay awake and close to God, each time will have less of an impact.

~Wow! Pow! Slap! ~

I got what I deserved! God truly opened my eyes to myself. On the bus this morning I encountered a hostel black man. This man looked maybe in his late twenties, early thirties maybe. This man hated and I mean hated black women! As he stated so eloquently, and I quote "Ewwww I hate black chicks" with pure disgust as he sat next to me. After making that comment he moved to another seat and continued to talk to a girl on the bus that showed in her face she was not interested in the conversation. To avoid this man acting up she humored him with a basic conversation. When the conversation came to a slow roar between them, he would look at me in disgust. This man began to make up a rap saying "I hate black bitches, die black bitches". This man continued his aggressive behavior with make-shifting his fingers into the shape of a gun and pointing at me while continuing his rap. Then punching the seat in front of him stating he wants to beat black bitches down. At one point I thought to myself this man's distain and disgust for black women (me) was just too extreme. This has gone too far and became too ridiculous! But just then I saw myself. Not the outer part of this man but the inner. This man was so transparent you could easily tell how he felt. I remember a time I felt that way. I BECAME SO ASHAMED OF MYSELF.

I am reminded of a story of a man I had the privilege of meeting once. This man had recently been released from prison for manslaughter. Trying to find comforting words for him, I asked what happened. The gentleman explained how he had gotten into a fight with another man over what he saw at this point to be foolishness. However, when it happened it seemed like something important to fight about. The gentleman stated as he and this other man were drinking upon leaving the bar, a fight started between them. The gentleman punched the other man causing him to stumble back. The man fell and hit his head on the corner of the curb, killing him instantly what a freak accident. So I said to him, it was an accident and you weren't at fault. The gentleman looked at me fighting back tears in his eyes as he stated, "My actions are responsible for that man's death, just the same as if I had put a gun to his temple and pulled the trigger. Just because I did not mean to do it, won't bring him back to life. My actions still caused his death."

Then I understood him, regardless of the intention the result was still the same. In the past I would say negative things about black men. Why? Lashing out because I was hurt that my own black men rejected me, so I waged war and rejected them. But what does the bible say about such talk?

<u>Ephesians 5:4 states this: 4-Let there be no filthiness nor foolish talk nor crude joking, which are out of place, but instead let there be thanksgiving</u>

Instead of just letting it go, I cradled and nurtured a hurt from too many years that had gone by. Not seeing that all men are not the same and you can't judge all by one or a select few. So, I thought I was punishing all but the only one that lost out was me.

This man on the bus seemed to have a deep seeded hurt from the women in his life, that should have shown him the most love. This I understand, rejection hurts and stays with you for a long time. Only God can fix those feelings. Now his hatred is for every black woman based on sight purely skin color. I have experienced White, Spanish, Asian and Middle eastern men hating me on sight simply for my color. Even showing disgust in their eyes, body language and expression on their face when having to speak to me. Never to the level of the man on the bus.

Sounds crazy, but I deserved it. Why? I asked God to reveal things to me that would hinder me in service to Him. Jehovah opened my eyes and that morning on the bus that gentlemen, this African American man that said he doesn't like black bitches. That he hates black chicks, "Ewww" as he said while looking at me. I did nothing wrong to that man. No prior knowledge of him as well as no history with him. I didn't look at his face, praying to God at that moment He told me to keep my head down and continue to read my book. I believe God didn't want me to say something and aggravate this man any further. I could care less about his behavior, only that it opened my eyes about me. However, I was concerned for him spiritually. I knew I needed to pray for him and repent for myself. I would never want anyone as well as myself to lose the blessings of God based on me not listening and obeying Him. I don't want anyone to miss out on that. However, I am not going to put myself in a situation that I know is not a safe or a spiritually unhealthy one. Definitely as in this one where he was irrational and hostel, I could not feed into that. I knew God was trying to teach me a lesson. A lesson I wanted to learn even though it was hard to see myself this way.

I thought I was over these feelings of distain for black men. Although I love my people, black women and men, I still had a bit of distain for black men within me. Sad to say it was my own people, black guys that criticized me and saw me as ugly. Never given a chance to get to know me, I conditioned myself to hate them as I felt they hated me. Early in life I wrote them off, not as friends but as lovers. I made excuses to push these men as far away from me as possible. For fear if they were close I would get hurt, as I had in the past. I was against them because I loved them so much. Although I didn't have my father, I did have brothers that I love. I looked up to them. Dreaming of the day all six would walk me down the aisle on my wedding day. A bitter sweet feeling. I believe God was showing me how I had acted toward black men, so I could repent. My actions were not to the level of the man on the bus, extreme but I feel the way it affected others was the same. The people on the bus were very uncomfortable and when I made comments in the past I know I made people uncomfortable because it was wrong.

~Dark to Light~

I enjoyed having a dark personality in the past, I really did it made me feel empowered. Feeling bigger than I was, like no one could touch me. I thought I was safe and secure because I put on that persona, that façade. It made me feel safe. Feeling so out of control, this negative way that I adopted for my life. I accepted the inner hurt I felt constantly, this dark mean personality made me feel powerful. I enjoyed the darkness of my personality. This allowed me to think I was better than other's, smarter, prettier and more talented.

Reality check, NO! I wasn't. I didn't come close or even touch many others' that I felt I was better than. Now I find that personality to be heavy, cumbersome, depressing and hurtful. With that dark personality came a behavior that allowed me to be lazy, dragging. It allowed me to have no focus, no ambitions, no future, just a whole lot of arrogance. I love this light hearted person that I am now. I love smiling and laughing and interacting with people. I'm still trying to do this, I'm still at the beginning stage of all this but I know this is the person that God intended me to be. A more lighthearted, laid- back, educated, analytical type of person, that is approachable at all times comfortable in her own skin. The go-getter that God wants me to be, the person that is always readily available to help someone else. I think that's the person I'm supposed to be because of God's love and His word the bible.

Psalms 119:92   92-If your law had not been my delight, I would have perished in my affliction

~In Conclusion~

This book wasn't written to make me look good or to make me look bad. The goal of this book is to help young ladies that feel that maybe they've done so much in their lives that they are at a point of no return, a point I came dangerously close to. At a point were the thought is, "God can't possibly love me not, after the life I have led." Ladies that are at a place in there lives where they want a relationship with God, but feel their past makes them unworthy. This book is to help women to understand God was always there for them then and He will be there for them now. He's not judging you, but He will help you to see a better life. The life that He, Himself has planned for you. The life that was meant for you from the beginning. At some point in our lives, we get derailed. We look for things on our own, always trying to stand on our own knowledge of what's best for us. But as the bible states in:

Proverbs 3:5-8 5-Trust in the Lord with all your

heart, and do not lean on your own understanding. 6-In all your ways acknowledge him, and he will make straight your paths. 7-Be not wise in your own eyes; fear the Lord, and turn away from evil. 8-It will be healing to your flesh and refreshment to your bones

When we don't follow God's words, that's when we get into trouble. That's when we go the wrong way, that's when we come into contact with all the hardship. And all the misfortune that we really don't need to go through. The things that we could've avoided. If we had just listened to our Heavenly Father. I write this book not to make me look good, because it doesn't. I have made many mistakes I am not proud of. It's not to make me feel dragged down or feel like garbage. It's so that something that happened in my life, the way I was living my life hopefully can help someone else in their journey to find God. To not just find God, but to also serve Him.

My only love, my only want, my only concern, is to serve God. His way, for me is the only way. God took me from a place that was so dark, so damp, so disgusting and it was as if I could physically feel it on me. I had made life so bad for myself, I could feel the slime of life on my body. No matter how hard I scrubbed, the feeling of the gritty stench would not come off. God turned that around for me, He cleansed me, refreshed me and made what was old, renewed. For so many years the enemy brainwashed me to believe my life was just fine and I was living to the most I could. That meeting men and hoping for the best was the way it was to be. The thinking of the world was this, it's just the way it is, you can't change it. Or the saying I hated to hear the most was, "You have to kiss a bunch of frogs to find a prince". No, no you don't! God's way assures the right person for you. The man that God has prepared just for you. Ladies, we are all special and God is the only one that can provide us with that special spouse and life just for us in His service.

SCRIPTURES USED:

Introduction -	1Corinthians 6:20
Ok, where do I start? –	Deuteronomy 5:16
Becoming Tara -	
Relationships -	1Corinthians 6: 18-20
	1Corinthians 7: 13-14
.	Ephesians 5: 22-33
Circle Time -	
Fornication/Sexually -	1Corinthians 6: 9-10
Immoral	1Corinthians 6:18-20
	Matthew 6: 24
Another piece of the - puzzle	1Peter 5: 8

Drawing a line -

Past view on men -

Show and Share (explicit) -

Animal −

Better -   Mark 9: 43-47

My Testimony -

Presentation -   Proverbs 24: 16

                                   Matthew 6: 8

Hot Mess -   1Peter 5: 6-7

                                   Ephesians 1: 7

Mr. Right -   Psalms 37: 7

                                   Matthew 6: 8

                                   Proverbs 3: 5

My Condition -

Side Chick -	Matthew 6: 8
Depression -	Psalms 43: 5
	James 1: 22-24
	2 Corinthians 12: 9
Packages -	Galatians 5:22-23
Amusement park -	Ecclesiastes 7: 12
Afro -	Lamentations 3: 40
Back in the day -	Ephesians 3: 16-19
Giving it away -	John 10: 10
Red rover Red rover -	2 Corinthians 2: 11
Wow! Pow! Slap! -	Ephesians 5: 4
Dark to Light -	Psalms 119: 92
In Conclusion -	Proverbs 3: 5-8

*Bible used

English Standard Version (ESV)

Made in the USA
Middletown, DE
16 September 2015